NATURAL NUTRITION for CATS

Also by Kymythy R. Schultze, C.N., C.N.C.

NATURAL NUTRITION FOR DOGS AND CATS:
The Ultimate Diet

THE NATURAL NUTRITION NO-COOK BOOK:
Delicious Food for You . . . and Your Pets!

Hay House Titles of Related Interest

YOU CAN HEAL YOUR LIFE, the movie,
starring Louise L. Hay & Friends
(available as a 1-DVD program and an expanded 2-DVD set)
Watch the trailer at: **www.LouiseHayMovie.com**

CAT COMFORT CARDS, by the staff at Hay House

COMMUNICATION WITH ALL LIFE:
Revelations of an Animal Communicator,
by Joan Ranquet

NATURAL HEALING FOR DOGS AND CATS A–Z,
by Cheryl Schwartz, D.V.M.

All of the above are available at your
local bookstore, or may be ordered by visiting:

Hay House USA: **www.hayhouse.com**®
Hay House Australia: **www.hayhouse.com.au**
Hay House UK: **www.hayhouse.co.uk**
Hay House South Africa: **www.hayhouse.co.za**
Hay House India: **www.hayhouse.co.in**

NATURAL NUTRITION for CATS

The Path to Purr-fect Health

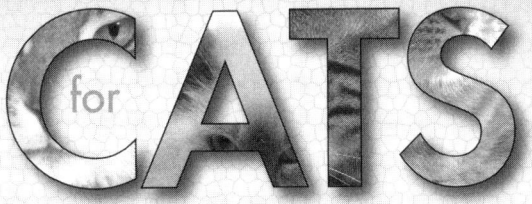

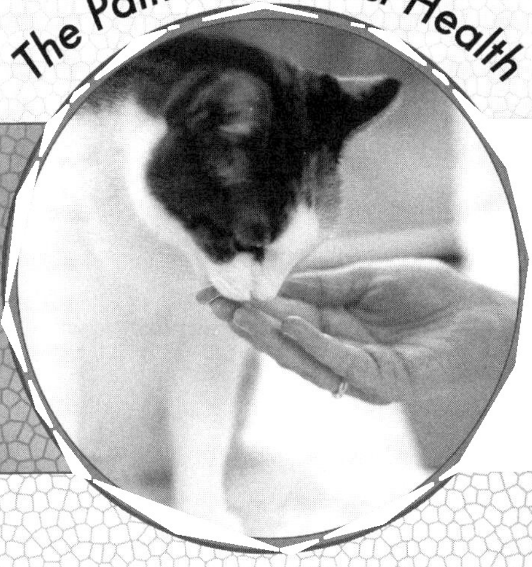

Kymythy R. Schultze, C.N., C.N.C.

HAY HOUSE

HAY HOUSE, INC.
Carlsbad, California • New York City
London • Sydney • Johannesburg
Vancouver • Hong Kong • New Delhi

Copyright © 2008 by Kymythy R. Schultze

Published and distributed in the United States by: Hay House, Inc.: www.hayhouse.com • **Published and distributed in Australia by:** Hay House Australia Pty. Ltd.: www.hayhouse.com.au • **Published and distributed in the United Kingdom by:** Hay House UK, Ltd.: www.hayhouse.co.uk • **Published and distributed in the Republic of South Africa by:** Hay House SA (Pty), Ltd.: www.hayhouse.co.za • **Distributed in Canada by:** Raincoast: www.raincoast.com • **Published in India by:** Hay House Publishers India: www.hayhouse.co.in

Editorial supervision: Jill Kramer • *Design:* Amy Rose Grigoriou

All rights reserved. No part of this book may be reproduced by any mechanical, photographic, or electronic process, or in the form of a phonographic recording; nor may it be stored in a retrieval system, transmitted, or otherwise be copied for public or private use—other than for "fair use" as brief quotations embodied in articles and reviews—without prior written permission of the publisher.

This material has been written and published for educational purposes only. The reader understands that the author and publisher are not engaged in rendering veterinary advice or services. The author and publisher provide this information, and the reader accepts it, with the understanding that people act on it at their own risk and with full knowledge that they should consult with a medical professional for medical help. The author and publisher shall have neither liability or responsibility to any person, pet, or entity with respect to any loss, damage, or injury caused or alleged to be caused, directly or indirectly by the information contained in this book.

Library of Congress Cataloging-in-Publication Data

Schultze, Kymythy R.
  Natural nutrition for cats : the path to purr-fect health / Kymythy Schultze. -- 1st ed.
     p. cm.
  Includes bibliographical references and index.
  ISBN-13: 978-1-4019-1072-3 (tradepaper) 1. Cats--Nutrition. 2. Cats--Food. I. Title.
  SF447.6.S38 2008
  636.8'085--dc22

2007038957

ISBN: 978-1-4019-1072-3

11 10 09 08   4 3 2 1
1st edition, March 2008

Printed in the United States of America

*For my Button . . .
until we meet again.*

*Thank you to my furry family
for being such generous,
loving, gifted teachers and friends—
I'm a better human because of you.*

*And especially
to my husband Blair,
you're my superhero
(like Spidey, only <u>better!</u>)*

CONTENTS

Foreword by Cindy Geisler, D.V.M ix

Preface: The Evolution of Change
for the Better xiii

Introduction: Welcome! xxi

Chapter 1: What Is Good Health? 1

Chapter 2: Species-Appropriate Nutrition 11

Chapter 3: Your Cat's Nutritional Needs:
The Basics...................................... 21

Chapter 4: Kibbles and Cans and Cats . . .
Oh My! 33

Chapter 5: Artificial Preservatives 49

Chapter 6: What's in the Bag? 59

Chapter 7: Turning Up the Heat..................... 73

Chapter 8: Responsibility................................ 83

Chapter 9:	To Boldly Go Where Millions Have Gone Before 91
Chapter 10:	Let's Go Shopping! 115
Chapter 11:	Making the Switch 125
Chapter 12:	Special Needs and Life Stages 135
Chapter 13:	Use Caution with Cats 143
Chapter 14:	C.A.T. Diet Recipes 151
Chapter 15:	Holistic Health Care 161

Afterword 169
References 175
Resources 181
Index 187
About the Author 193

FOREWORD

by Cindy Geisler, D.V.M

"This book is a must-read for anyone who wants to learn more about pet food and improve their cat's health through better nutrition."

Every once in a while, someone emerges as the forward-thinking pioneer of a new paradigm. In the mid-1990s, Kymythy Schultze appeared on the scene as one such individual, and her trailblazing work in the field began a true revolution in animal nutrition. She was the first to recommend a grainless diet for cats (in her 1997 book *Natural Nutrition for Dogs and Cats*); her now widely accepted diet was truly ahead of its time. She built upon the foundational work of raw-feeding proponents Juliette de Bairacli Levy and one of my mentors, Dr. Richard Pitcairn, but questioned the value of the large amount of grain in their recommended diets. Because Kymythy's nutritional advice is biologically sound and achieves great results, many of the other experts in the field of animal nutrition have since revised their texts.

I met Kymythy in 2002 when I attended one of her wonderful lectures. She's an extremely articulate and passionate speaker; and her diet guidelines are science based, logical, and well organized. She isn't preachy and admits that her recommendations aren't for everyone, but once you hear her speak on the subject, the common sense of her reasoning is obvious. She has an enormous amount of care and empathy for the well-being of all animals, which drives her to do everything she can to help give them a better quality of life.

I once joked with Kymythy that she was the "Queen of Raw." Now I'm calling her the "Queen of Change" for having the courage to write about the unhealthy relationship between the pet-food industry and the veterinary community—and advocating for reform in the status quo. The pet-food recalls should be a wake-up call for every cat lover. Kymythy is determined to be a conduit for a change for the better, positively affecting millions of wonderful furry beings that count on us to do the right thing and make the best decisions for them. I'm very excited that she's now offering her wealth of knowledge to all of us. This book is a must-read for anyone who wants to learn more

Foreword

about pet food and improve their cat's well-being through better nutrition.

In my practice, I see many felines with diet-related health problems. I'm very pleased that I'll now be able to recommend this book for straightforward, accurate, and easy-to-understand answers to my clients' health and diet questions.

PREFACE

The Evolution of Change for the Better

"The greatness of a nation and its moral progress can be judged by the way its animals are treated"
— Mahatma Gandhi

Although it may give my age away, I'll admit that as I write this Preface, the song "Aquarius" is running through my head. In case you don't remember the play or movie *Hair,* the song was an anthem for revolution and change. Unfortunately, I know why the tune is on an endless loop in my mind: It's a reaction to the thousands of cats that are now dead or will be soon due to eating toxic products. One of the biggest pet-food recalls is happening at the very moment I'm typing these words. But don't be fooled—this is far from the first such incident in history (in fact, the recall average is more than one per year during the last decade). It's just that this is a really big one, so people are angry and blame is flying. The toxins that have been found have changed and multiplied so many times that it's hard to know who and what to believe. The pet-food companies' marketing and public relations people are on hyper-drive smoothing things over. After all, there are billions of dollars at stake—*their* billions.

Only one thing is certain: Laboratory analysis has confirmed that more than 100 different pet-food products contain one or more ingredients that can kill your beloved animal friend. The brands range from the cheapest to the most expensive "veterinarian recommended" ones. We'll never know the full extent of the damage done or how many animals died without anyone connecting it to the food they ate. And if the cats didn't die right away, we won't be sure whether the toxins in their food may have contributed to their deaths in the future.

It's Personal

I feel that I relate to this tragic situation in a very personal way. In addition to wanting good lives for all creatures—and especially being an advocate for animal wellness—I, too, had to endure immeasurable pain and suffering before my health improved.

Preface

(Of course, I'm alive now, so I'm more fortunate than some of the cats affected by the recall.)

I came into this world with numerous health issues. Even as a newborn, I had to have excruciating injections for anemia, and from there the trips to the doctors and specialists seemed to take up a large part of my life. By the time I was an adult, I'd been diagnosed with multiple sclerosis, allergies, wry neck, skin problems, bone loss, torn nerves, arthritis, TMJ disorder, a heart murmur, chemical poisoning, hypothyroidism, celiac disease, and fibrocystic breast disease. And those are just the ones I can remember!

Life was looking pretty grim until I wheeled into a new doctor's office one day (I couldn't walk well by then and was frequently using a wheelchair). I must admit that I had every expectation that Dr. Richard Dahout wouldn't be any different from the rest, who hadn't offered much relief beyond writing prescriptions for painkillers and such. But this physician, who had a family practice that focused on nutrition, *was* different. He was actually excited about my challenging case and was eager to help me!

After a thorough examination, instead of prescribing the usual painful procedures, he began teaching me how to eat a better diet. It wasn't a radical program, simply a way to supply my body with the nutrients it needed to heal and be well again. There weren't any weird ingredients or concoctions, just fresh, unprocessed food that's appropriate for the human body, with a few tweaks for my particular health problems. I was fascinated, and his passion for good nutrition was infectious. At first, I was still skeptical, but at that point I had run out of options, so I decided to go for it.

I'll never forget "day ten" of following my new eating regime. It was then that I realized that the painful lumps in my breasts were *completely gone!* About a year earlier, when I'd been diagnosed with fibrocystic breast disease, a different doctor had said that the medical profession didn't know what caused it or how to cure it. I was told that the lumps would hurt more and more over time and that I just had to learn to live with it. So you can imagine my joy when the pain disappeared! And I continued to feel better as my body responded to eating more nutritious food. Soon, I was up walking again and enjoying life—I was beyond amazed! And I bet you can understand now why I have a passion for good nutrition.

After my experience, I was extremely motivated to find out more. I devoted myself to learning all that I could about proper nutrition. And since

Preface

I've always felt responsible for my animal friends' health and happiness, my drive included discovering how to improve their health as well. *After all,* I thought, *if simply eating better could make such a wonderful difference in my body, think of the benefits my animal family might enjoy.* I dug deep and studied animal nutrition as well as human.

I was blessed that my wonderful doctor became my mentor. With a knowing smile, he'd call me a trailblazer and patiently answer my many questions. I believe that he appreciated my intense drive to learn about the right foods for animals because it paralleled his own passion for human nutrition.

Being a wildlife rehabilitator for the federal government also helped in my study of natural wild-animal diets. I've traveled the globe and spent countless hours learning about food and nutrition. To say that it's been an interesting journey would be quite an understatement. And this journey is never ending, for new information is always just around the next corner.

Learning how to feed our furry companions a proper diet for better health was—and still is—so very important to me. Animals have always been a special part of my life. In my darkest moments, they've been there for me with unconditional love and companionship; during times I really felt that it was too physically painful to go on, they gave me the strength and motivation to keep trying. In addition, they're incredibly enlightened beings and have so much to teach us. Sharing my life with them is a joy and privilege.

The Furry Nut—My First Cat

El Pecan was his name—just Pecan to his friends—about whom he was very selective. He was a huge (of course, I was very small at the time) long-haired black cat with big golden eyes, and he was my introduction into the wonderful world of cats. He was my best friend when I was a little girl, and his companionship was just what I needed at the time. When I was stuck indoors, he entertained me for hours by running and leaping like a madman, zooming around the house. And at night, he curled up on my pillow, and we fell asleep, breathing together in rhythm. He actually took up most of the pillow, but I didn't mind.

I've lived with many wonderful cats since then, but I'll never forget my Pecan and how much that big ol' tom meant to a little girl. He made me feel safe and loved at a very crucial time in my life. His memory and my continuing love of cats motivate me to learn and share information to help them all enjoy a great quality of life. I don't want anyone—children or adults—to lose their best friend any sooner than they have to.

Change for the Better

The pet-food recall is why I can't get that old song out of my head. I have to believe that a change for the better will come out of this unforgivable disaster. I have to replace the pain in my heart with my knowledge, experience, and passion for helping our animal friends live the healthy lives they so richly deserve. That's my path for this life and my mission for this book: to help you feed your cats a diet that they'll thrive on. We're not aiming for okay here—we're going for *great!* And guess what? It's doable!

If you're interested in providing a better diet for the health of your feline companion, join the revolution! Let's take more control of our dear cats' health and diminish their discomforts. I *know* that change for the better can and does happen—I've lived it—so "Let the Sun Shine In"!

INTRODUCTION

Welcome!

*"Read not to contradict and confute;
nor to believe and take for granted; nor to find
talk and discourse; but to weigh and consider."*
— Sir Francis Bacon

Keep your paws and tail inside the bus; our journey is about to begin. But first, I want to express sincere respect and gratitude to you for taking the time and effort to learn how to better care for your feline companion. I don't take it for granted, because we all know there are far too many animals that don't have concerned caregivers. Even if this book isn't your particular cup of tea, I still admire your desire to help your cat. In this case, curiosity may indeed save that cat!

In this book, I won't demand that you do anything or try to frighten you into feeding your cat a certain way. I'll simply take you on the path that I followed when I first began preparing my own cats' meals at home more than two decades ago. I'll provide you with information about nutritional needs and processed pet-food products and give you suggestions on how to prepare a nutritious homemade meal for your feline friend. Certainly, different opinions abound in the field of nutrition for cats just as they do for humans, but common sense and an open mind will help guide you.

A good diet for your cat is one that provides the correct nutrients, in the proper forms, that it needs to be healthy and happy. Plus, the regimen has to please you, too. If you're uncomfortable with a particular way of feeding or if you don't understand it, you probably shouldn't be doing it. How you feed your cat must fit into your personal comfort zone and be good for your cat as well. I realize that even though all felines are the same species, each one is also an individual—and so are you! Because of this, I'll offer you a few different types of diets to choose from. Even though I certainly know which is right for me and my cats, you may make a different choice.

My goal is to present you with a broad scope of important information. Then you'll have the freedom to make diet choices for your cat that are doable for *you*. Of course, when you've finished reading this book, I do hope that you'll choose to follow

Introduction

my favorite diet suggestions. But even if you pick my second or third recommendations, I still feel that they'll benefit your cat's health much more than a processed product. The main goal here is to get some real food into your feline friend!

The reason I'm so adamant is simple and heartfelt: I've known so many cats that have blossomed into radiant health by eating the way that I suggest in this book. After numerous years of helping cat lovers improve their furry friends' diets, I've had the great pleasure of receiving wonderful and sometimes amazing feedback regarding their animals' increase in health. At my seminars, there are often lots of happy tears and hugs when people relate how their cats overcame terrible health issues after eating the diet I recommend. And of course, my own cats have done exceedingly well on this diet for the past two decades. If they didn't, I wouldn't do it! Please keep in mind that diet is not a "magic bullet"—it is the most important part of your cat's health plan.

If you choose to feed differently than is suggested in the following chapters, I still commend you for seeking nutritional guidance and suggest that you can nevertheless use some of the information to help you make diet decisions that you're comfortable with. And I hope that you'll continue your education and learn more about cat care. At the end of the day, no matter how you choose to feed the cat in your life, I thank you for your compassion. Just the fact that you've spent the time and effort to read this book tells me that we really do share the same goal: We want to increase the health and well-being of our beloved feline friends so that they can be with us—happy and healthy—for as long as possible.

CHAPTER 1

What Is Good Health?

"Of all God's creatures, there is only one that cannot be made slave of the lash. That one is the cat. If man could be crossed with the cat it would improve the man, but it would deteriorate the cat."
— Mark Twain

Unfortunately, health problems have become so prevalent in cats today that many people have begun to accept these disease states as "normal." Some veterinarians see unwell animals so frequently that even they've come to take these conditions for granted as simply the "usual" issues that cats have. Perhaps we've forgotten how a truly healthy feline should act, look, and feel.

Problems with skin, coat, parasites, teeth, weight, odor, digestion, kidney, thyroid, pancreas, diabetes, urinary, respiratory, and immune systems are *not* normal. They're not signs of good health! A healthy cat has a strong immune system to fend off disease. It has a glossy coat with a wonderful texture and pleasant smell, along with clean teeth and breath that doesn't knock you over. A healthy cat has a digestive system that utilizes the food it eats and deposits small stools in its litter box. It doesn't have bad hair days; flaky skin; or constant problems with fleas, worms, and hair balls. It doesn't have urinary blockages, and it has behavior appropriate for a healthy cat.

According to many individuals who feed their cats a species-appropriate diet (we'll talk about what that is in upcoming chapters), the benefits are numerous and the most common increases in health include:

healthy skin and coat	fewer parasites
normal digestion	no bad odor
improved behavior	better quality of life
reduction/elimination of hair balls	no urinary problems
	better mobility

What Is Good Health?

> better stools
>
> clean teeth
>
> increased energy
>
> no allergies
>
> ... and many more!

Following are just a few of the too-many-to-count comments that fellow cat lovers have made to me. I know how they feel—when I first switched my cats over to a species-appropriate diet of real food, their health increased dramatically. I was so ecstatic that I wanted to share it with the world to help other cats! It's certainly understandable that others feel the same, and if you're like me, you'll enjoy sharing a connection with other feline fanciers. Personally, I'm interested in their journeys and especially enjoy stories with happy endings. I like knowing that a cat's suffering has ended and its health has improved. Often, there's something valuable to be learned; and even if there isn't, I like getting to know other people and their furry family members. And I really love finding out what people have named their cats or—as is often the case—what name the cat has chosen for itself.

Vito and Julius

Vito is a long, lean black cat with lovely silver shading; and he has a mane like a little black lion. When Sarah adopted him, he was a mess. He had a potbelly full of worms, fleas, poor digestion, smelly ears, a head tilt, and the nasty habit of pulling out all the fur on his belly. After switching him from the cat "chow" he came with to the diet recommended in this book, his health problems resolved beautifully—he no longer needs a toupee for his underside! And he's an absolute piggy when it comes to mealtime.

His housemate Julius is one of the most handsome tabbies I've ever seen. Sarah adopted him as a very tiny kitten and fed him the raw diet right from the start. His coat is so plush and glossy that you just have to touch it. Sarah also notes that both cats smell very nice, and a great bonus is the fact that they've never needed to go to a veterinarian for any illness, so she saves money in that area. Both boys are so healthy and vibrant that as Vito approaches 16 and Julius nears 20 years of age, they're often mistaken for youngsters.

Halley, Emma, Socks, Strider, and Jaggers

Fiona, who lives in Scotland, thought she was doing the right thing by following her veterinarian's advice to raise her kittens—Halley, Emma, Socks, Strider, and Jaggers—on the "scientifically formulated" premium commercial cat food that he sold at his clinic. As the cats matured, however, they began to suffer from various ailments, including urinary crystals, cystitis, and kidney failure.

When Socks was diagnosed with cancer, Fiona placed an order to the U.S. for a copy of my first book. After reading it, she immediately went out and purchased the ingredients to begin feeding her cats a species-appropriate diet. All of the cats took to it right away and proved to Fiona that feeding a more natural diet was definitely the way to go.

Fiona has since started her own crusade to help educate others. After much research, she concluded that feeding processed pet food is causing serious illness and death in our cats. She's made such a convincing case that the president of the Royal College of Veterinary Surgeons in London has asked her to meet at the House of Commons to discuss the problem of pet-food companies being allowed to fund and teach nutrition at veterinary schools. And she's currently following up on a lawsuit against some of the biggest of these corporations for making false claims for their products. It sounds like we may be hearing more from Fiona in the future—you go, girl!

Molly Mayonnaise

While co-workers display photos of spouses and children, Joyce is such a cat lover that she has pictures of Molly on her desk at work—and yes, the cat's full name is Molly Mayonnaise. I love cat names, don't you? Joyce switched her beloved cat over to the diet in this book when Molly was eight years old. She was motivated by her feline companion's lack of interest in commercial cat food, her dull coat, and her decrease in energy.

Joyce found a butcher that grinds free-range, organic turkey breasts and chicken necks. She started to transition Molly to the new diet by adding a little of it to her commercial food, but Molly skipped the old stuff and went right for the raw food. Joyce reports that her cat's beautiful black coat and overall disposition have greatly improved, and they're both happy with the change. She also notes that she goes to a health-food store for pets where all of the employees feed their animal companions a raw-food diet.

Clarence and Rosalind

One of Susan's two cats (Clarence and Rosalind) began having urinary-tract blockages about eight years ago. After two trips to the emergency vet due to Clarence's difficulty urinating and blood in his urine, she was told to place him on a processed pet food for urinary problems. As Susan didn't feel comfortable doing this, she decided to feed him a raw-food diet. Within weeks he was back to normal and has been extraordinarily healthy ever since, without any recurrence of urinary problems.

When kitten Rosalind joined the family, she weighed just two-and-a-half pounds, having been found abandoned at four weeks of age. Susan fed her the raw diet right from the start; and today Rosalind is a beautiful, healthy cat. Susan now goes to a veterinarian who fully supports the feeding of raw-food diets to pets and recommends it to other clients. Susan has now written a book and occasionally gives seminars on healthy pet diets.

Jasper, Matilda, Salte, and LeRoy

Erica came to one of my seminars back in 2001. She decided to switch her cats Jasper, Matilda, Salte, and LeRoy to the species-appropriate diet of raw foods, but they had other ideas. She admits that at first she was a pushover and the cats knew it, of course. When they balked, she gave them kibble again. But when she became really determined to make the change, it took only a week before they were eating their new diet with gusto and licking their bowls clean. They love crunching on whole bones and have beautiful teeth to show for it.

Her recommendation to other newcomers is that once you're ready to feed the new diet, just do it —and stick to it. She's convinced that you need to be confident with the new diet for the cats to eat it. She also offers reassurance that it only gets easier, and in no time you'll be like her: happy you switched and wondering why you didn't do it sooner.

By making a large batch of food and freezing it in smaller containers, Erica finds feeding this way to be very easy. The health benefits her cats have experienced since eating the raw diet include a low-odor litter box, improvement in weight and muscle, less shedding, better breath, and drinking much less water (as cats should). Erica sends us a lovely toast: "Here's to a kibble-free house and healthy, happy animals, including us!" I extend my personal thanks to Erica for caring enough to rescue these wonderful cats from the facility where they were scheduled to be euthanized.

Your Cat's Name Here

All of the above cats and many others have enjoyed wonderful health benefits from eating a diet of raw, fresh foods. Each cat guardian has chosen methods for preparing meals that suit their needs and lifestyle. Even though their methods may vary—such as making big batches of food and freezing the extra or preparing meals daily—they all find it a very doable way of feeding their feline friends. And even though what they prepare varies slightly (some give bones whole, some don't, and so on), all their cats have enjoyed better health.

In the following chapters we'll discuss the why and how of preparing nutritious meals so that your cat may also enjoy the benefit of better health. Perhaps we'll share your success story in the next edition of this book!

CHAPTER 2

Species-Appropriate Nutrition

"In my 34 years as a holistic veterinary practitioner, I've found that optimum nutrition is the foundation for all methods of healing, whether alternative or conventional."
— Stephen R. Blake, Jr., D.V.M.

So what's the big deal about food? Why does it have such a huge influence on a body's health? Well, simply put, food is body fuel. It nourishes each and every cell and creates the energy necessary for life to happen. It's an overly simplified analogy, but food is to living beings like gas is to cars. If you put the wrong type of gas in a car, it won't run well; if you put in the correct fuel, it runs better.

Next to air, food is the substance our cats take into their bodies most often. How long they live, their quality of life, the health of their immune system, and their behavior all depend greatly on what they eat. Food is the foundation for health. It's really no different from what we hear today about *human* health. The experts keep telling us that if we wish to live long and healthy lives, we need to eat more real food and cut out the processed products.

It seems that every day there is new research to support this advice. Fresh food, with all its wonderful array of nutrients intact, provides better "fuel" than processed products that have had their nutritional content altered or destroyed and may include many deleterious substances that actually work against good health. As both humans and felines have strayed from eating fresh foods, both our species have suffered a huge increase in obesity, diabetes, allergies, cancer, behavior problems, general ill health, and more.

These days, there are so many bottles of nutritional "supplements" on the market and so many processed fake foods that perhaps we've forgotten that real, fresh foods are the original and best source of all those vitamins, minerals, enzymes, antioxidants, and other important nutrients necessary for good health. Even now, malnutrition is still a very real issue for cats (and humans). Malnutrition puts a great deal of stress on the body and lowers the energy needed to maintain good health. It may be caused by lack of food, poor quality food, or food cats can't utilize because they're not appropriate for the species *Felis domesticus*. When I began my quest to provide the best diet for my own feline companions, I wanted to know just what their bodies were physiologically designed to thrive on.

Food Fit for a Cat

To understand what food is best for our cats, we need to know what their anatomy is designed to best utilize. Bruce Cauble, D.V.M., puts it very succinctly when he says, "Animals, just like people, are still using digestive systems that evolved thousands of years ago, systems designed to provide them with nutrients derived from whole foods. You need only look at the digestive system of an organism to determine its appropriate diet." Please read that last sentence again because it very clearly sums up the proper way to feed our cats. Yes, it's that simple: We need to look at how evolution has shaped the structure of the cat.

When you have the chance, take a good look at your cat. It has needle-sharp teeth and claws meant to catch, hold, and tear flesh. It has ears that face forward and eyes in the front of its head to better focus on that mouse or bird it wants to chase. Those potential meals are built differently. Being prey animals, they usually have eyes more to the sides of their heads, in order to better see who's trying to make them into lunch! Your cat's digestive system is brilliantly designed to eat specific foods. It's short and acidic; proper foods are utilized swiftly and efficiently. That snuggly-wuggly kitty in your house is actually a well-developed predator.

Officially, the cat is a carnivore. Webster's dictionary defines carnivore as any of an order (Carnivora) of fanged, flesh-eating mammals, including the cat. Every aspect of your cat's body, inside and out, is that of a beautifully designed, predatory carnivore. In fact, your cat is actually an *obligatory* carnivore, which means that it must eat meat. Just because it resides in your home and enjoys your company doesn't change its physical makeup and its nature. And simply because it may not be providing its own meals every day as it would in the

Species-Appropriate Nutrition

wild doesn't change what type of food it needs to thrive. It requires species-appropriate food—that is, a diet that its body is designed to utilize well in order to be healthy. Obviously, it shouldn't eat the same things as a cow or a chicken because that's not how it's designed. Cattle and chickens are herbivores and are structurally quite different from your cat.

All those feline attributes mentioned before—the teeth, claws, eyes, ears, and digestive system—are designed to eat specific foods. What foods? Other smaller animals, of course! If your cat has ever caught a rodent or bird, then you've been given a perfect example of what it's meant to eat. Now, I'm not saying that you must place a live mouse in your cat's dinner bowl (although some cats would love it), but we do need to offer food that matches what they were built to eat as closely as possible. That's the responsible thing to do when you've chosen to live with a carnivore.

On its own, the cat would eat its food raw. A mouse never comes precooked! The natural diet would also include many parts of the prey: bones, organs, and the like (depending on the prey animal and the predator's personal preferences). How do they tolerate *raw* meat? Nothing could be more natural and familiar to their bodies. Remember that brilliantly designed digestive system? It's short and acidic. That way, the cat gets the raw meat in, it's digested quickly before any possible negative bacteria multiply, and what's left over is excreted.

By the way, raw meat does *not* always carry negative bacteria. Many zoos and captive habitats have been feeding their wild cats raw meat and bones for years because they discovered that the animals just didn't thrive without it. And remember, our house cats are still the same inside as those untamed cousins.

When we supply our cat's body with species-appropriate "familiar" types of food, the body knows just what to do. It's able to utilize all the nutrients it needs, with very little waste left over. As our cat's guardian, we should respect the true needs of the animal we so dearly love.

Domestication?

Science can trace our cats' heritage back about 120 million years. It's said that the species was domesticated perhaps 4,000 years ago (a blink in time, really). At that point, they were very useful in helping keep the rodent population down around human habitats. Over the centuries, they continued

Species-Appropriate Nutrition

to contribute their skills at "pest" control everywhere from palaces to working farms, ranches, granaries, and other places where their predatory abilities were needed and appreciated.

Keeping cats as indoor "pets" is a relatively new practice. For the majority of our history with them, they've mostly been outdoor predators, eating their natural wild diet. We shouldn't be surprised then as we watch our indoor kitty display all the qualities of a small tiger! I'm sure you've seen a wild cat in a zoo or such and noticed the similarities to your feline friend at home.

I'll never forget the time I watched a mountain lion leap across my path (I lived in the mountains at the time). It took my breath away! It was big, it was well muscled, and it was most definitely a cat. Another wild cat I've had the pleasure of watching in its natural habitat is the beautiful bobcat. I enjoyed living in an area with such wonderful creatures, but I don't think my mother's Jack Russell terrier felt the same when a bobcat tried to carry her off one day. Talk about role reversal—a cat's revenge on the dog! Thankfully, my mom's dog is fine and now stays closer to home.

Both of those wild animals are really just larger versions of our house cats. And in many ways, it's debatable whether our cats are really a lot more "domesticated" than their larger cousins. But isn't that one reason we love them so? Living with cats gives us a close connection to nature, and we're privileged to share a bond with a creature still so "wild."

Certainly, we've developed special relationships with our feline friends, but they do retain much of their untamed heritage. Most "pet" cats have little trouble securing their own food when left outside or becoming feral. Of course, with today's many environmental hazards, it's not recommended that a beloved cat be left outside to fend for itself. That's why it's up to us as responsible guardians to provide a safe living place and proper nutrition, in a form that's as natural and species appropriate as possible.

In the next chapter, we'll discuss your cat's specific nutritional needs—and Jack Russell terriers aren't on the menu!

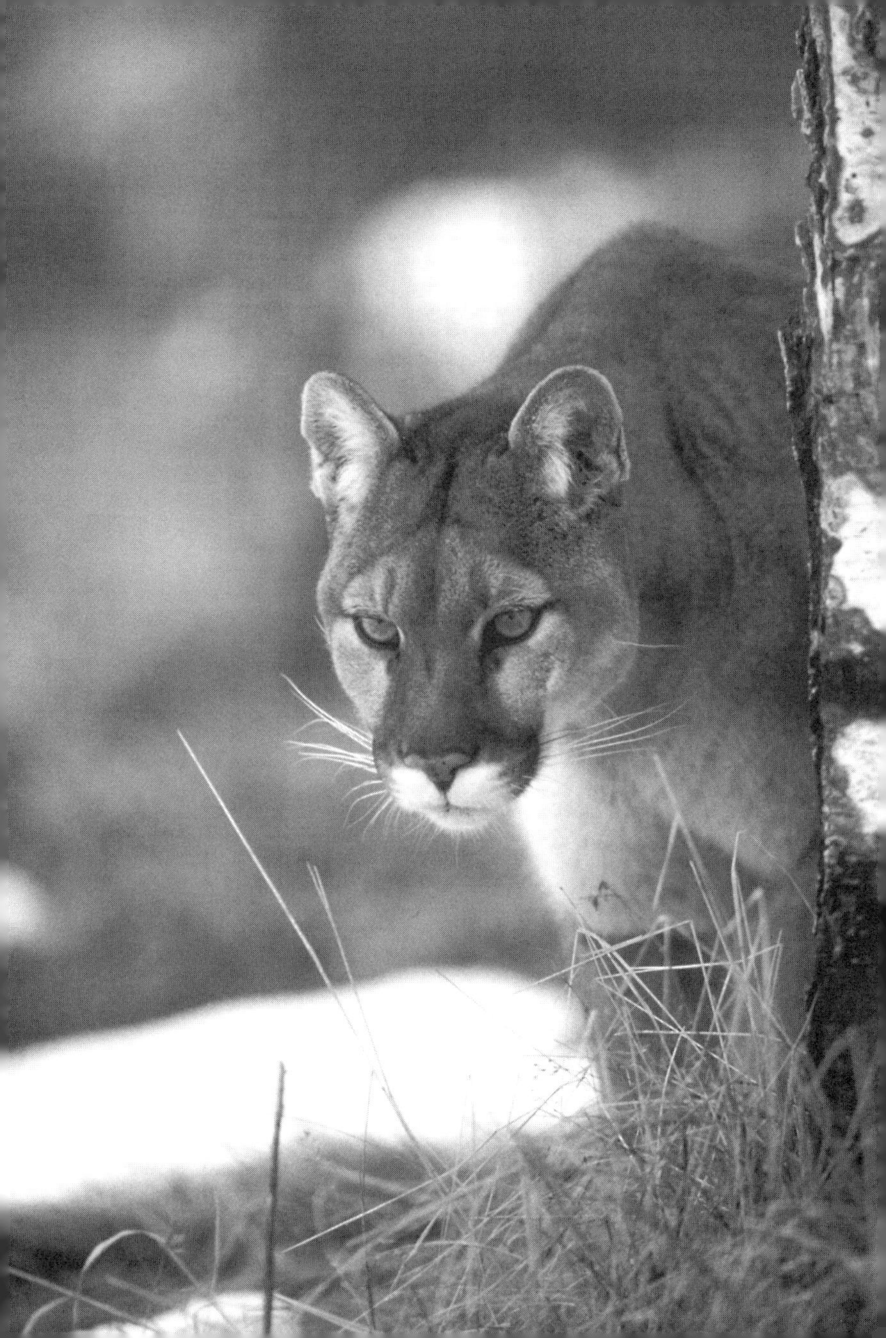

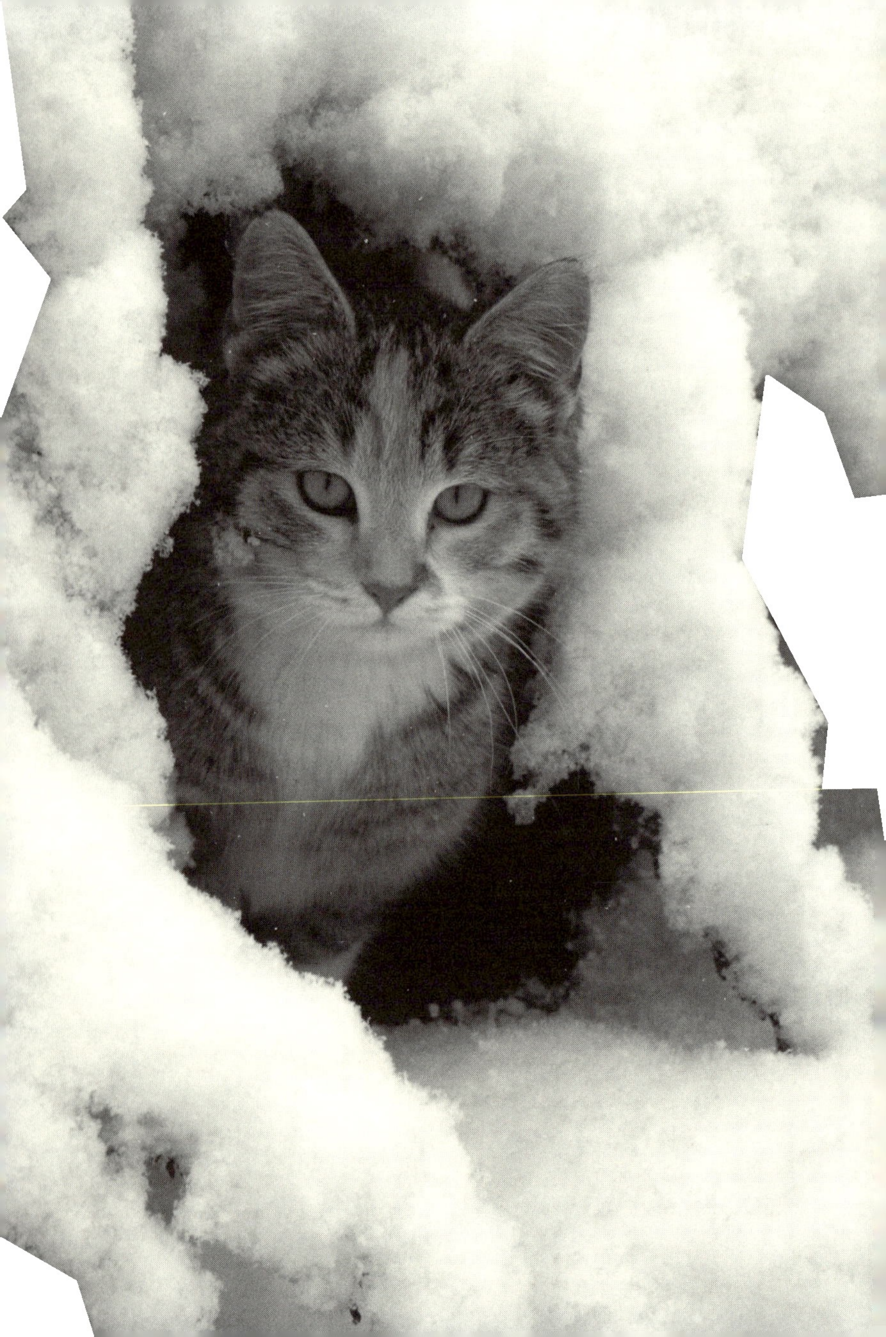

CHAPTER 3

Your Cat's Nutritional Needs: The Basics

"After dark all cats are leopards."
— Native American proverb

This chapter discusses the basic nutritional needs of your cat. Many nutrients have been studied individually in a clinical setting—in fact, they're examined more individually than in the food they came from. This is unfortunate because it's important to remember that the essential building blocks of health aren't isolated in nature. Whole foods contain a complex blend of synergistic compounds that work together to support optimal well-being. While that may sound complicated, it really isn't—if you simply use species-appropriate real food as the foundation for health.

One of the great things about feeding our cats a well-prepared diet of real food is that it's chock-full of all the nutrients we know are important to feline health. Plus, we're also including natural nutrients that have yet to be isolated, synthesized, and added to the cans and bags of processed pet food. It's more complicated for pet-food manufacturers who formulate products with isolated ingredients to make an appropriate substance that mimics real food in supporting a lifetime of great health.

Take the taurine disaster, for example. Taurine is an amino acid that pet-food manufacturers didn't consider essential until cats begun to suffer and die from eating processed products deficient in it. Now it's an isolated chemical added to most cat foods, but if you're considering feeding your cat *real* food, I have great news: The first food group we'll discuss is a fantastic source of natural taurine!

— **Protein.** Dietary protein supplies essential amino acids and is needed for the manufacture of antibodies, enzymes, hormones, and tissues and for proper pH balance. It provides energy for cats and is essential for growth and development. Complete proteins contain ample amounts of essential amino acids and are found in foods such as meat, fish, eggs, and poultry. Incomplete proteins do not provide all essential amino acids and are found in many foods, including legumes, grains, and vegetables. These plant proteins don't supply the essential amino acids that a cat needs (such as taurine), which come from animal protein.

Cats need animal sources of this nutrient, as the amino acids from vegetable sources aren't well utilized. How much each animal may need can vary slightly due to a variety of factors, including physiological state, age, activity, and the digestibility of the protein source being fed. Overall, cats have a very high requirement for protein.

— **Fat.** This concentrated source of energy also provides essential fatty acids and aids in nutrient utilization and transportation. It's involved in cell integrity and metabolic regulation as well. Saturated fat is found primarily in animal sources, while polyunsaturated fat comes mostly from plants.

Fats (and oils) are composed of fatty acids, sometimes referred to as "vitamin F." The following are the fatty acids most involved in feline health:

omega-3 fatty acids, which include alpha-linolenic (ALA), eicosapentaenoic acid (EPA), and docosahexaenoic acid (DHA); and omega-6 fatty acids, including linoleic acid (LA), gamma-linolenic acid (GLA), arachidonic acid (AA), and conjugated linoleic acid (CLA).

Linoleic and arachidonic acids have long been considered to be essential fatty acids (EFAs) for cats. More recently, DHA has been added due to its important contribution to feline vision, reproductive health, and the immune system. EPA may also be of benefit.

Essential fatty acids are just what they sound like—essential for the cat's health—and they must be obtained from food sources. Unlike some animals, felines don't efficiently convert plant sources of EFAs to the needed derivatives. For example, cats *must* eat meat to obtain arachidonic acid. Also, they don't convert LA to GLA (as some animals do), and studies show that GLA can benefit the health of feline skin and coat. We can theorize that in nature, the cat would eat another animal whose body had already made the conversion, thereby offering some of this useful fatty acid. The cat would also consume omega-3s and CLA when eating its natural herbivorous prey.

To sum up, LA; AA; DHA (which is mostly found in nature with other useful omega-3s); and to a lesser extent, EPA and GLA, can be considered important fatty acids for good feline health. CLA may become recognized as a bigger player in feline nutrition in the future because it's found in the meat and fat of a cat's natural diet, but it has only recently been "discovered" by nutritional science.

— **Minerals.** These are essential to the cat and are involved in almost all physiological reactions. They contribute to enzyme formation, pH balance, nutrient utilization, and oxygen transportation and are stored in bone and muscle tissue. Biological availability may vary widely depending on the source of the nutrient. Elemental minerals are generally taken from the earth or water; chelated minerals are those that are bound with other organic substances, often making them easier for the body to absorb.

Minerals include calcium, chloride, chromium, cobalt, copper, fluorine, iodine, iron, magnesium, manganese, molybdenum, phosphorus, potassium, selenium, silicon, sodium, sulfur, and zinc. There are others that cats require at trace concentrations. Minerals, like vitamins, work synergistically, with a cooperative action between them.

— **Vitamins.** These nutrients are essential for metabolism regulation and normal growth and function. Usually found in food, some are synthesized within the animal's body. They're classified as either fat or water soluble.

Fat-soluble vitamins include A, D, E, and K. The water-soluble group includes C and the B complex. Generally, fat-soluble vitamins are stored in the body, while water-soluble ones pass through more quickly. Once again, the carnivorous cat utilizes animal sources of nutrients more readily than plant sources. For example, felines can't convert beta-carotene from plants into vitamin A (as some animals do), so they need preformed vitamin A from an animal source. This type needs no conversion.

— **Water.** Because cats are designed to fulfill most of their water requirements by eating fresh raw food, they naturally have a low thirst drive. This can lead to health issues when they eat dry food products and treats. One of the problems is that even though they become dehydrated eating the kibble, their natural "programming" may not encourage them to drink more, and their urine can become too concentrated. Even though a healthy cat doesn't drink much, you should always have clean drinking water available. And please make sure it's good quality, which means that just turning on the faucet may be out, especially if your community puts fluoride in the water supply. If you have a well, get it tested annually for contaminants.

But Wait . . . There's More!

There are a number of other substances that contribute to good health, some of which come from food sources and some of which are created within the body. These include antioxidants—comprising vitamins, minerals, and enzymes—which help protect the body from damaging free radicals. Now, I know that "free radicals" sound like a terrorist group, but they're actually cell-damaging atoms. Hmm . . . I guess you could consider them a form of body terrorist! Free radicals may be formed internally by exposure to cigarette smoke, pollution, radiation, and other damaging substances. With our cats being bombarded with more environmental toxins than ever before, antioxidants are important factors for good health.

Enzymes are protein molecules that are essential for most bodily functions. They're involved in energy, tissue, organ, and cellular repair and much more. They're also essential for digestion, and different species of animals need different levels for particular types of food. Not surprisingly, creatures have the enzymes needed to properly break down the foods found in their natural diets and tend to be deficient in those that work on substances they wouldn't eat in the wild.

In addition to being manufactured by the body, enzymes can also be found in food, although temperatures of 118 degrees or above destroy them. Those in raw ingredients help prevent depletion of the body's internal supply of enzymes.

There are probably many more nutrients yet to be discovered, but that's the great thing about feeding fresh food—those undiscovered, yet important, substances are already in there!

What's Not Nutritionally Required

You may have noticed that carbohydrates (usually supplied by grains in pet food) weren't listed among the necessary nutrients for cats. Even the National Research Council's Subcommittee on Cat Nutrition states that ". . . no known dietary carbohydrate requirement exists for the cat . . ." And really, if you consider feline physiology and what the species has been eating for thousands of years, it makes perfect sense that grains shouldn't be part of the cat's diet.

Another good reason not to feed grain is the fact that it breaks down into sugar within the body—something a cat definitely doesn't need! Many studies link sugar consumption to illness, including cancer. Eating a high-carb diet really wreaks havoc on a cat's body. Carbs are usually thought of as energy foods, but felines utilize protein and fat very efficiently for those needs. This is one reason why cats have such a high requirement for quality protein.

Good Nutrition Is a Team Effort

All the components we discussed don't work alone in nature; foods don't contain single nutrients. For example, we've probably all heard that oranges are a good source of vitamin C, but that piece of fruit contains many other cofactor nutrients that actually aid in the absorption and utilization of the vitamin. Even if farmers created a "Franken-orange" that contained only that vitamin, it wouldn't be as effective without the other "helpers," such as bioflavonoids and minerals that aid in vitamin C's effectiveness.

Likewise, vitamin E isn't simply the d-alpha-tocopherol that you'll find in a capsule from the store. It's actually a family of at least eight different molecules that work better when taken together, the way they're found in fresh food, rather than alone in supplemental form. Many studies have shown that natural nutrients from food are more beneficial than isolated synthetic supplements. And by the way, oranges aren't a species-appropriate source of vitamin C for cats, but raw liver is.

Nonfood Requirements

Your cat has other needs in addition to a good diet. Yes, food is the foundation of health, but there are other factors that can have a big impact on your feline friend's well-being. Of course it needs a clean, accessible litter box and a safe place to call its own, but your cat also needs *you*.

Even though cats are perceived as very independent creatures, they really do benefit from your love and attention. Please talk to, play with, and touch your cats in ways they enjoy. I promise that if you make them an important part of your life and treat them with love and respect, you'll all benefit immeasurably.

In the next chapter, we'll take a look at who's benefiting from the formulation of processed pet-food products—and who isn't.

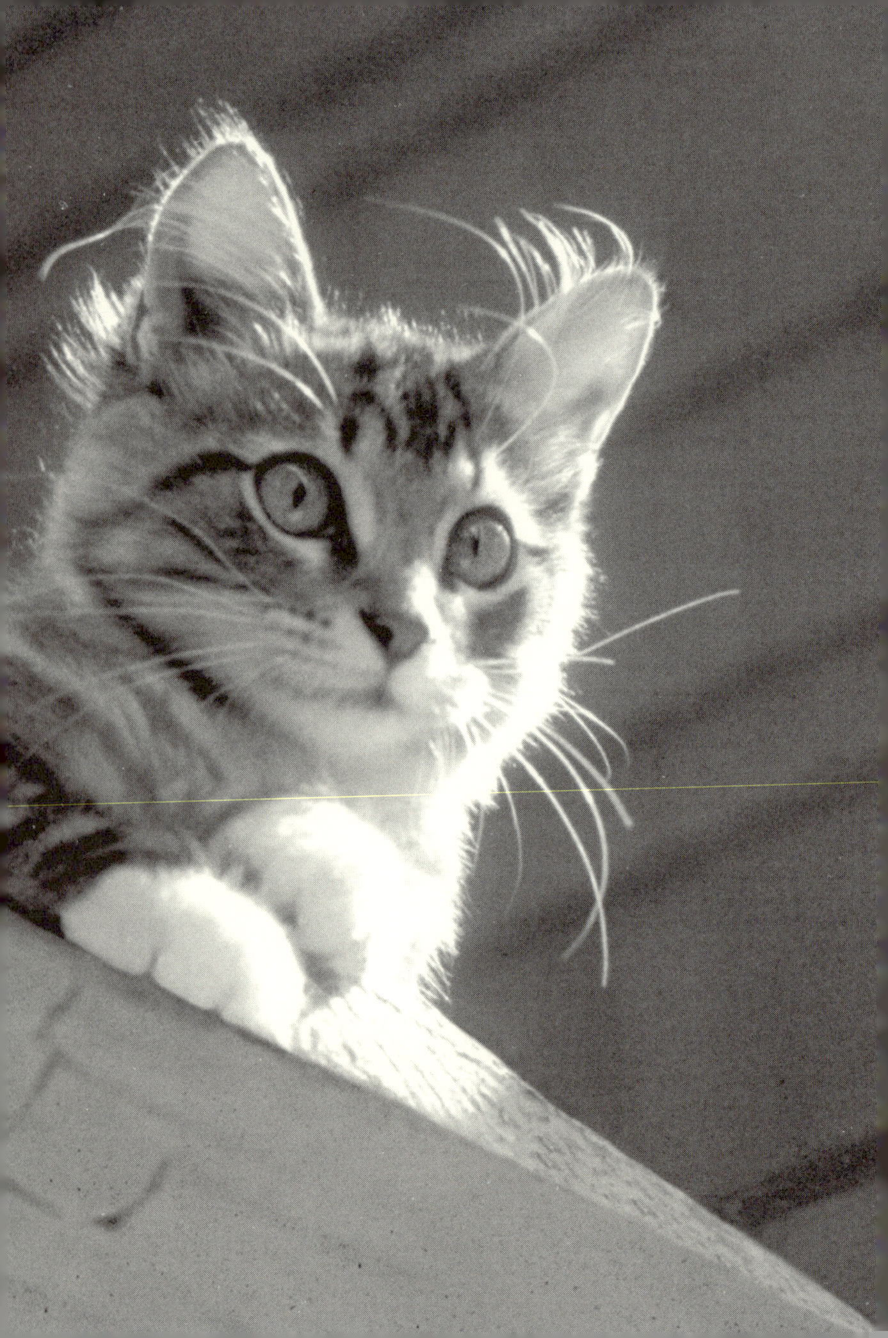

CHAPTER 4

Kibbles and Cans and Cats ... Oh My!

"As anyone who has ever been around a cat for any length of time well knows, cats have enormous patience with the limitations of the human mind."
— Cleveland Amory

In my quest to learn how to best feed my feline friends, I wanted to find out how commercial cat-food products were made—how they were formulated and exactly what sorts of ingredients they contained. (When I look back, I find it amazing that I'd used them for many years without really knowing much about them.) I wanted to discover more about my feeding options so that I could feel comfortable with whatever I decided was right for my cats.

How Pet-Food Products Are Formulated

The pet-food market is big business—*really* big business. We're talking many billions of dollars each and every year. With all the various brands out there, you'd think there'd be a lot of different corporations in the game, but there aren't. Sure, more small companies are popping up these days to grab a piece of the pet-food pie, but the majority of the market is still dominated by just a handful of players. And as we've learned with the recent recall, most of these companies actually have their products made by the same manufacturers. Many of the major pet-food makers are subsidiaries of multinational corporations that also make human products. This gives them the opportunity to take better advantage of marketing, buying power, and business affiliations; and it gives them an outlet for their waste materials.

Guidelines for pet-food products are created—not regulated—by the National Research Council (NRC) and the Association of American Feed

Control Officials (AAFCO). One would assume that they've thoroughly researched our cats' every nutritional need. After all, the labels on each can and bag promise that the product is "complete and balanced" for a cat's life because it met that expert criteria. I used to assume that was true. I was surprised when I actually read the NRC's book *Nutrient Requirements of Cats*. If you haven't seen it yourself, I'll share a bit of what it contains.

Inside you'll find the results of nutrient experiments and recommendations for what cat-food manufacturers should include in their formulas. They also have a section on suggested ingredients. Okay, so that doesn't sound too bad, right? Wrong. I actually found a lot that concerned me.

First off, in the Preface, they explain that they don't have information about many nutrients (and looking through the book, that sure is true!), so for the ones lacking any data for cats, they've recommended *minimal* (not optimal) quantities or made estimates based on experiments with *other species!* In fact, all throughout the book, many feeding suggestions for the cat are based on studies using rats, chickens, dogs, and pigs, even though the NRC states that a cat's needs are unique and are quite different from other laboratory animals. The authors actually say, "Few nutritional requirements are known for the adult cat for maintenance or for pregnancy and lactation."

They also acknowledge that some of their stated values probably aren't minimal requirements and that energy estimates based on caged cats should be interpreted with caution. It should also be noted that many of these nutrient experiments were based on felines eating purified diets (lab chow made specifically to include or exclude specific nutrients). Under the mineral heading, they admit that cats definitely need minerals, but they don't have much data on the qualitative or quantitative requirements. Basically, the same is said about vitamins: Very limited research has been done.

Now, let me state something quite clearly: I actually appreciate the fact that they admit they don't "know it all" regarding the cat's nutritional requirements. The book isn't trying to deceive me; it states over and over how little the experts actually know. But—and it's a big "but"—I do *not* appreciate the extremely deceptive practice of pet-food companies stating that their product is "complete and balanced" for my cat's life, based on the research performed. That statement is simply not true. According to their studies and methodology, it can't be.

In addition to the nutritional information being incomplete, pet foods aren't tested over a cat's entire lifetime. Well, actually cat lovers are doing that work right now on their beloved felines by feeding these products, and so far the results for many cats haven't been very good.

I want to mention something else that you may not be aware of in regard to most of the official studies done to determine the cat's nutritional requirements: the cruelty involved. I know it's not a pleasant topic, and I don't enjoy discussing it. But I also know that before I began my investigation into pet-food products, I didn't know about the extent of this practice, and perhaps other folks don't either. I'm not talking about animal testing for pharmaceuticals or such—that's a different topic that warrants an entire book itself. No, I mean the insane cruelty that takes place simply to determine what nutrients a cat does or doesn't need or what food it will or won't eat.

When I was studying animal nutrition at Cornell University, I had to endure continual references to these cruel studies and even a slide show depicting the gut-wrenching results. And I don't think I'm being overly sensitive, especially in regard to the slides showing how young animals were terribly deformed after their mother was intentionally deprived of calcium. The professor proudly exclaimed that they'd discovered that calcium was a necessary nutrient. I wanted to scream "Well, duh!" Of course it's a necessary nutrient! A simple look at a cat's natural diet—or, dare I propose, just using your brain—would reveal that.

On television we see commercials with happy kitties and kindly people feeding them products that are devoured immediately. We're made to believe that the pet-food companies care about our cats as much as we do. That's marketing, folks. Now, I'm sure many individuals in the biz do love animals, but in fact, one of the really big companies was brought under fire a couple of years ago when evidence was uncovered that exposed their horrible product-development tests on animals. And they aren't the only company that does this kind of thing.

I won't give you the gruesome details, because if you're like me, they'll make you extremely nauseated and angry. I'm okay with the angry part, though, because that's often how things get changed for the better. The part that upsets me the most is the fact that animals don't have to be tortured and killed to find out what's good for them to eat. We certainly don't do this sort of testing on our human children to determine their recommended daily allowance of nutrients (RDAs), and it doesn't have to be done on our feline family members either.

Official Product Testing

Originally, companies were required to conduct feeding trials in order to claim that products were "complete and balanced," but AAFCO devised a way around that expensive procedure. The latest method for a product to get to tout that it's "complete and balanced" *without any form of testing at all* is the newer "family rule." This allows the company to claim the product is "similar" to one that *was* tested. But you and I have no way of knowing what the original item was or just how similar the new one is to the old one.

Although they aren't used as often as they used to be, some feeding trials are still conducted. But the question remains: Does the process prove that a product will support optimal health for my cat's entire lifetime? In a feeding trial, a minimum number of cats are fed a product for a minimum amount of time—it could be a couple of weeks to a few months. This research is especially unpopular with makers of cat-food products because felines tend to be more finicky than other animals. Within these studies, a number of subjects are allowed to be removed due to poor food intake, illness, or other reasons. There could be no nutrient requirements for the product being used in the trial, so in theory, it might be quite unbalanced. But as long as it sustains a minimum number of cats for a small period of time, it's deemed "complete and balanced" for the entire life of my cat. Quality of life and longevity aren't part of the test, and even a yearlong feeding trial may not expose imbalances that take longer to affect a cat.

Another way a product earns the "complete and balanced" statement is simply by chemical analysis. Unfortunately, this doesn't tell us if a cat will be able to digest, utilize, or even like the product. Plus, the acceptable amount of various nutrients is vast and can range from a few milligrams to a few *thousand* milligrams of a single substance. How can the products with the lowest and highest numbers both earn "complete and balanced" status?

What Is in Pet-Food Products?

Of course, not all cat-food products are made with the exact same ingredients, but in my search for information, I discovered that the majority of the popular ones I looked into contained very questionable ingredients. Unless they're vegetarian formulas—which are definitely *not* recommended for your carnivorous feline—they usually contain some form of animal protein. Parts of food animals that aren't used for human consumption, either because they're unpopular or are deemed unfit, are very popular ingredients in pet foods. A slaughterhouse employee told *Prevention* magazine: "I once worked in a chicken-butchering factory in Maine. Our average daily output was 100,000 chickens. Directly ahead of me on the conveyor line were the USDA inspectors and their trimmers. The trimmers cut the damaged and diseased parts off the chickens and dropped them in garbage cans, which were emptied periodically. These were sent to a pet food factory."

Yes, "4-D" (dead, dying, diseased, or disabled) animal parts are allowed to be used in cat food. These may include cancerous tumors, bowels, pus, hooves, beaks, ear tags (the plastic tags put on cows' ears that contain insecticides), fetal tissue, slaughterhouse waste, and other parts not consumed by humans. The Pet Food Institute—a trade association of manufacturers, not a regulatory association—feels these ingredients provide an important source of income to farmers and processors. I'm all for supporting farmers, but not at the expense of my cat's health! Anyway, the farmers aren't the ones creating a market for this waste from the human-food industry.

What can feeding such ingredients do to your cat? From his experience as a veterinarian and federal meat inspector, Dr. P. F. McGargle concludes that it increases their chance of getting cancer and other degenerative diseases. He's witnessed pet-food meats that were moldy, rancid, spoiled, and cancerous. Some of the scraps may contain hormone levels comparable to those that have produced cancer in laboratory animals. Cats are especially sensitive to this toxic load. Unfortunately, these hormones aren't destroyed by the high heat and pressure that pet-food manufacturing requires.

Do you ever wonder what grocery stores do with all their expired meat? Rather than being written off as a total loss, it may be sold to companies that put it into pet-food products. As it wouldn't be cost effective to remove the plastic wrap and Styrofoam, these are thrown into the protein mix along with the expired meat. Another undesirable protein that may be used—there's no law against it—is roadkill and dead pets. Of course, I'm certain every manufacturer would deny it, and I'm sure not every one of them would use these items, but there are some suspicious findings.

Baltimore's Valley Proteins rendering plant reports that they take an average of 1,824 pounds of dead animals from the local pound each year. They transform it into commercial meat and bonemeal, tallow, and grease. Not all of it winds up in your cat's dinner, but the plant says it does sell about 34 percent of its rendered material to pet-food companies.

Do you remember the segment on the TV show *Hard Copy* where a journalist followed a guy who was scraping roadkill into a truck in between stops at animal shelters, where he picked up euthanized cats and dogs to be brought back to the rendering plant? I do, and it caused a big uproar at the time! The scandal was such that the FDA conducted a study to see if they could find any pentobarbital, a common euthanasia drug, in pet foods. Unfortunately, they did. Even if manufacturers don't seem to use these "ingredients" today due to public pressure, there's still no law against them doing so.

Another major ingredient in pet-food products is grain. It creates texture and shape; helps hold the product together; and provide carbohydrates, filler, and vegetable protein. And it's a lot cheaper than meat! But there are quite a few flaws with this ingredient. Let's look at quality—or lack thereof—first. Much of the grain that goes into these products is nothing more than agricultural waste and scraps that are deemed "not fit for human consumption." Even old bakery products, which would otherwise be thrown out, make their way into pet food.

One of the biggest problems with the "not fit for human consumption" grains that are used is the contaminants they may contain, including mold, fungus, and aflatoxins. This last substance is formed from mold and can cause serious and even fatal liver damage. Unfortunately, the American Association of Veterinary Laboratory Diagnosticians has reported that "virtually all animal foods contain viable mold." Contaminated grains have been the reason behind quite a few pet-food recalls, including the latest one where a different toxin was discovered: melamine, which is used to make plastic and its by-products. Reports say that it was intentionally added to increase the protein analysis of the grain.

The most ironic and ridiculous thing about the grain in cat-food products is the fact that cats have absolutely no nutritional requirement for grain! It was mentioned before (and is worth repeating) that even the NRC's *Nutrient Requirements for Cats* states: "Although no known dietary carbohydrate requirement exists for the cat, dry commercial diets usually contain 40 percent or more. . . ." Cats aren't equipped to utilize a high-carbohydrate diet and it may lead to obesity, diabetes, urinary issues, and other serious health problems. Eating grain puts a tremendous strain on the feline body, and cancer cells definitely have a "sweet tooth" and thrive on the sugar that grains provide.

Then there are the "fat blenders." I didn't know such a business even existed until I began looking closely into pet-food product ingredients. Fat blenders are just what they sound like: They collect fats and oils from various sources, mix them together in big vats, and sell the goop to pet-food manufacturers. Their source material is usually rendered animal or vegetable fat deemed unfit for human consumption. If you've ever noticed a big barrel of used grease behind a fast-food restaurant, then you've seen one source of the rancid fat that's allowed in pet foods. The combined fats are often sprayed onto products that your cat would otherwise not want to eat. If that doesn't do the trick, manufacturers may add various flavors (artificial or natural) to the fat in order to convince the cat to eat it.

Creating Shelf Life

Every pet-food manufacturer has to consider their product's shelf life. Preservatives must be added to ensure that the item makes it from the manufacturer through distributors, storage, shipping, and sitting on store shelves and into your cat's bowl containing enough palatability for your cat to eat it. Preservatives can be added by the supplier of the individual materials, the manufacturer, or both. For example, a pet-food company may market their product by claiming they haven't added artificial preservatives—but they don't have to tell you that the fish meal they use is already heavily preserved with a potent artificial chemical before they purchase it.

A more recent trend you'll see today are products that claim they only contain "natural" preservatives such a vitamins C or E or various herbs.

While this may sound better, remember that the company doesn't have to reveal what preservatives were already used by their suppliers. Plus, while natural preservatives do sound like a good idea, they dissipate rather quickly and result in a much shorter shelf life.

We'll take a closer look at some of the preservatives used in pet foods in the next chapter.

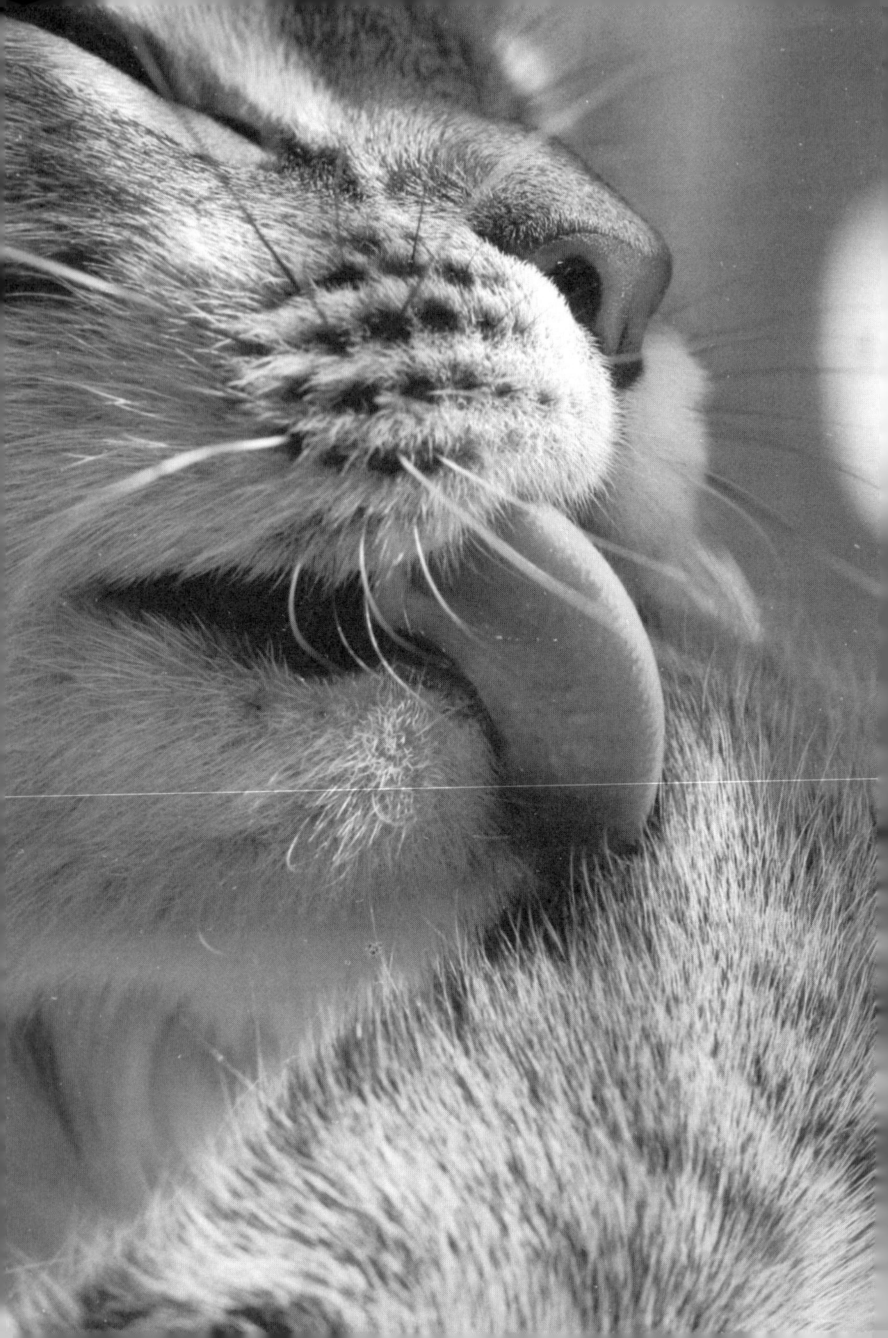

CHAPTER 5

Artificial Preservatives

"It is one of the miracles of science and hygiene that the germs that used to be in our food have been replaced by poisons."
— Wendell Berry

Let's delve a bit deeper into some of the more popular preservatives that are used in pet-food products. Many of these are highly frowned upon for human consumption, but are given the okay for animals. There are so many studies proving their toxicity that I'm blown away when I read them on pet-food labels. Of course, not all of these exist in every product, but many are used either by the manufacturer or the material supplier or both. Here are just a few examples of what you might find on the label of a processed cat-food product:

— **Artificial dyes and flavors.** Artificial colors are added to make pet-food products more pleasing to the human eye. They offer no benefit to our cats and are more likely to contribute to health problems. For example, Red 40 is used in food, medications, and cosmetics; it's associated with cancer in laboratory animals. Yellow 5 is linked to asthma attacks and urticaria (hives) in children. Blue 1 is banned in Belgium, France, Germany, Switzerland, Sweden, Austria, and Norway. Yellow 6 is related to an increase in tumors, allergies, and hyperactivity. Artificial dyes and flavors have been linked to nervousness, anxiety, hostility, allergies, and behavior problems.

A single artificial flavor may actually be a combination of hundreds of individual chemicals, many derived from petroleum. These ingredients have been shown to have deleterious effects on liver enzymes, RNA, and thyroid function. Most haven't been studied for safety and neurotoxicity, and some artificial flavors contain salicylates (related to aspirin), which can be fatal to cats.

— **Benzoic acid and related compounds.** These are used as food preservatives and antifungal agents. The problem is that they're not well metabolized by cats. It's important to note that benzyl alcohol can be used in lactated Ringer's solution (which is used when giving intravenous or subcutaneous treatments) and may cause poisoning in cats receiving fluids with this preservative. Sodium benzoate is a popular preservative, even in some "health" foods, but can be toxic to cats.

— **BHA and BHT.** These preservatives are used in food, packaging, cosmetics, rubber, and petroleum products. Studies have found that they induce double-strand DNA breaks, DNA adducts, mutations, and chromosomal aberrations. They increase the risk of tumors and have caused stomach cancer in lab animals. When heated to decomposition, they emit acrid and irritating fumes. They're also banned in some European countries. Strangely, in the United States, individual states are allowed to choose whether to label them as carcinogens (cancer causing) or not.

— **Citric acid.** This one doesn't sound too bad, does it? It can be used in food for flavoring, to increase acidity, as a firming agent, and as a preservative. It may be derived from citrus fruit, but most of the citric acid used is actually made from corn through the fermentation of crude sugars. One of the problems with it for many individuals is that some of the corn protein remains during processing; and, when it's hydrolyzed, it produces free glutamic acid (also known as MSG). Citric acid may also interact with other proteins, producing even more MSG. This is a very problematic preservative linked to many health problems, and we'll investigate it further in an upcoming section. Even if citric acid comes from a non-corn source, citrus fruits aren't recommended for cat consumption as they may cause gastrointestinal distress.

— **Ethoxyquin.** This chemical was originally developed as a rubber stabilizer. It, too, is banned in many countries. In the United States, it's only approved for human consumption in extremely small doses to preserve spices. But it's widely used in larger amounts in animal food, even though animal studies have linked it to sterility; deformed offspring; an increase in cataracts; and lesions of the liver, kidney, and bladder. It's a big enough health concern that in 1997, the FDA's Center for Veterinary Medicine asked that pet-food manufacturers voluntarily reduce the level being used by half.

Artificial Preservatives

Note that corporations weren't *required* to do this, but asked to make the change voluntarily. Ethoxyquin has never been tested for safety in cats.

— **MSG (monosodium glutamate).** MSG is often used as a flavor enhancer. It's an excitotoxin—a chemical transmitter that harms brain cells. It's also been linked to eye damage, fatigue, disorientation, obesity, and allergies. One would think that it would be easy enough to avoid MSG by reading labels, but unfortunately it's not that simple. In the United States, it's not required to be listed individually when it's part of another ingredient.

When reading labels, know that these substances usually contain this preservative:

MSG	hydrolyzed plant protein
monosodium glutamate	autolyzed plant protein
monopotassium glutamate	sodium caseinate
glutamate	calium caseinate
glutamic acid	textured protein
gelatin	yeast extract
hydrolyzed vegetable protein	yeast food or nutrient
	autolyzed yeast

These substances often contain MSG:

malted barley flavor	"enriched" items
barley malt	protein fortified
malt extract or flavoring	modified food starch
maltodextrin	rice or brown rice syrup
caramel	lipolyzed butter fat
soy protein or concentrate	low- or no-fat items
broth	corn syrup or solids
bouillon	citric acid from corn
wheat, rice, or oat protein	milk powder
whey protein or whey	dry milk solids
whey protein isolate or concentrate	protein-fortified milk
flavors, flavoring	annatto
reaction flavors	spice
natural meat flavors	pectin
soy sauce or extract	ultra-pasteurized
soy protein	protease enzymes
stock	enzyme modified
cornstarch	protease
flowing agents	fermented
carrageenan	gums
	dough conditioners
	yeast nutrients

— **Propyl gallate and propylene glycol.** Propyl 3,4,5-trihydroxybenzoate is an ester formed by the condensation of gallic acid and propanol. It's used to preserve fats and oils; it's also found in cosmetics, hair products, adhesives, and lubricants. It often appears in conjunction with BHA and BHT. Some studies suggest that it may contribute to cancer. It can cause liver, kidney, and stomach damage and contact dermatitis in some individuals. Its long-term safety for cats hasn't been studied. However, increased numbers of Heinz bodies (small, irregular, deep purple granules in red blood cells due to damage of the hemoglobin molecules), which may lead to hemolytic anemia, have been observed in cats eating diets containing propylene glycol.

— **Sodium nitrite and sodium nitrate.** These are mainly used to preserve meat and meat by-products, helping them keep their color (which I'm betting my cats don't really care about). During digestion, these chemicals form carcinogenic nitrosamines, which have been linked to an increase in many cancers, including those of the stomach, brain, nose, and throat. They're also associated with increased risk of leukemia, diabetes, respiratory infections, abdominal pain, and muscle weakness. As far back as 1956, they were discovered to cause liver tumors in laboratory animals; and they're banned from food use in many European countries. In addition to their use as preservatives, they may also contaminate well water. This has lead to fetal retardation and "blue baby syndrome" in infants given formula made with such water. Sodium and potassium nitrates are also used as fumigants to kill underground rodents.

— **Just a few more** . . . Well, we've covered several of the more popular preservatives. According to many sources, including the Animal Protection Institute, other additives that may be used in pet foods include: anticaking agents, antigelling agents, antimicrobials, curing agents, drying agents, emulsifiers, flavor enhancers, grinding agents, humectants, leavening agents, lubricants, palatants, pelleting agents, binders, petroleum derivatives, pH-control agents, seasonings, spices, stabilizers, sweeteners, texturizers, and thickeners.

Artificial Preservatives

Coming up, we'll examine the label of a popular cat-food product. And even though the ingredients appear to be listed for all to see, we now know that there may be other substances present, such as preservatives and additives, which we won't find in the fine print.

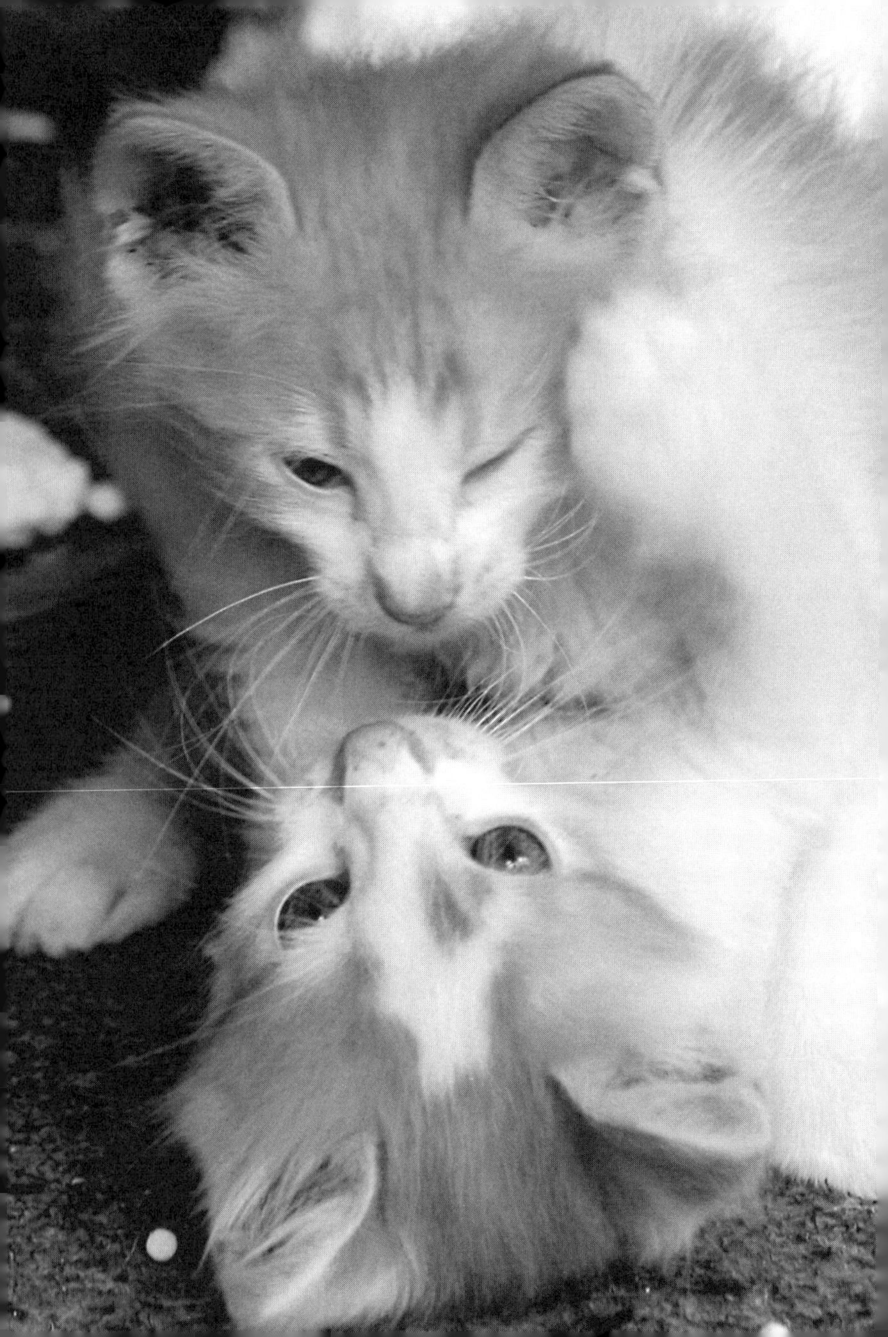

CHAPTER 6

What's in the Bag?

"People that hate cats will come back as mice in their next life."
— Faith Resnick

Let's take a look at the ingredients on the actual label of a dry cat-food product. I examined one of the leading brands that's quite pricey and sold through veterinarians. It boldly states that it's "veterinarian recommended" so it sounds like it must be very good for my cat. Now I could have easily evaluated one of the cheapo generic brands since one would assume that it would contain lesser-quality ingredients, but I went for a product considered to be among the very best for my feline family. This is an adult maintenance food, and the label adds that it's an advanced antioxidant formula. It sure does sound good!

The ingredients are listed in descending order of weight. We'll cover them in the order that they're listed on the bag:

— **Chicken by-product meal.** Well, shoot, we're not exactly starting out on the right foot here. I would much prefer a whole-animal protein to be the first ingredient. But whole meats are more expensive for manufacturers to use than lesser-quality by-products. By-products are the leftovers from the human-food industry, the parts not wanted by humans or condemned as unfit for our consumption. Chicken by-products may include feet, undeveloped eggs, necks, organs, and perhaps a few feathers. Now by-products aren't always bad, but the trouble is that we have no way of knowing the quality of this batch or the actual composition. They could very well be from 4-D animals. If the label said "meat," at least we'd know that it was the actual protein-rich meat of the animal, but by-product content and quality vary so greatly from batch to batch that we have no proof of what's really in this ingredient. By-products aren't necessarily bad for cats, who do naturally eat many animal parts that we may not care for. But having this listed as the very first ingredient instead of whole meat doesn't assure us that we're getting good-quality protein. The word *meal* means that it's been ground or pulverized.

Actually, the most disturbing fact about this ingredient is that it's the *only source of animal protein* in this product. And an abundance of high-quality animal protein is one of the most important dietary requirements for cats. One might think it reasonable to assume that the premium price of this brand of food and the fact that it's sold through veterinarians would assure us of better-quality protein. But I suppose the lesson is: Don't assume!

— **Cornmeal.** Wow, the very next ingredient—and therefore a large component of this food—is a grain meal. It's ironic that throughout history we valued cats for guarding our granaries against rodents. It was a good system because the felines didn't eat the grain. Now, pet-food manufacturers have discovered a way to get our cats to eat those very foods they would otherwise avoid. Corn isn't well digested by our carnivorous cats and can be very allergenic. There's absolutely no nutritional need for this ingredient. Its presence helps boost the overall protein analysis of the product, but it's vegetable protein, which isn't well tolerated or utilized by felines. Corn isn't a species-appropriate source of nutrients and may cause much stress to the cat's system. It's just not equipped with the enzymes and other factors needed to properly process cornmeal.

Another major concern is the fact that most corn in the U.S. is genetically modified. We're now learning just how dangerous this practice can be to animal bodies (both ours and our cats') and the environment. As if that's not enough, corn is a major source of dangerous aflatoxin—the reason behind many pet-food recalls because it's quite deadly.

— **Brewer's rice.** More grain! This is basically a waste product of the alcohol industry. It's the dried extracted residue of rice from the manufacture of wort (the liquid portion of malted grain) or beer, and it may also contain spent hops. The ASPCA considers hops to be poisonous to cats; ingestion may lead to an increase in heart rate, temperature, seizures, and in large enough quantities, even death.

— **Animal fat (preserved with BHA, propyl gallate, and citric acid).** Animal fat is a very generic term and can indicate poor quality. And after the high-heat processing and rendering that occurs during manufacturing, it would probably be more accurate to call this ingredient rancid animal grease. The unpleasant smell that many pet-food products have is partly due to the spoiled fats. To make matters worse, artificial preservatives are added that may harm our cats. (Please see Chapter 5 for more information about preservatives.)

— **Corn gluten meal.** More corn! When you add up all the grains in this product, they certainly outweigh the animal protein. This product is beginning to look more like chicken feed than cat food!

Corn gluten meal is the dried residue from corn after the removal of the starch and germ (here, the word *germ* refers to the most nutritious part of the plant, not a bacteria, virus, or the like). Corn gluten meal is a by-product made from the manufacture of corn starch or corn syrup or by enzymatic treatment of the endosperm (that last word isn't exactly what it sounds like either—it's food for the growing plant).

Corn gluten meal is very high in nitrogen and is a great weed killer. It helps boost the protein contained in pet-food products, although there's no guarantee that our carnivorous cats can actually utilize this form of vegetable protein. And again, it's important to consider that most corn is genetically modified and may contain aflatoxins. These extremely dangerous toxins are produced from mold and fungus; their ingestion is linked to liver damage, immune deficiency, increased susceptibility to infections, and other serious health problems. Heat processing or freezing doesn't kill aflatoxins; and unfortunately, pet-food manufacturers aren't required to test for it.

This is one of the ingredients involved in the current pet-food recall, and recent reports confirm that contaminated corn gluten meal has killed several furry family members.

— **Chicken liver flavor.** Notice that the label doesn't list actual chicken liver, just the "flavor," and it doesn't tell us if this is artificial or natural. It would be nice if more meat were involved instead of a sprinkle of flavoring used to convince our cats to eat a product they might not want otherwise. Many "flavors" contain the excitotoxin MSG.

— **Taurine.** Adding the amino acid taurine is the big thing now in cat-food products. Not too long ago, it was found that a deficiency in this nutrient caused fatal heart disease and blindness in cats. These terrible conditions happened to many cats eating "complete and balanced" products. It may have occurred because so little animal protein is used in many of them as they've become more grain based (it's a cheaper ingredient than meat). Plus, taurine is damaged by the heat used in manufacturing. So after the expense and suffering of many cats and their people who put their trust in these "veterinarian recommended, complete and balanced" products, the industry has now begun to add taurine to cat foods. That's very nice of them, but what other essential nutrients are missing from these products? Tomorrow they may discover another needed ingredient, but I sure hope our cats don't have to pay the price—again.

— **BHA and BHT.** Here are more of these dangerous preservatives. BHA has already been listed as being used to preserve the animal fat, and now they've added even more of these undesirable chemicals. (Please refer to Chapter 5 for more information.)

— **Beta-carotene.** This carotenoid acts as a precursor to vitamin A. When beta-carotene is ingested by some animals, the liver converts it to the vitamin, which is an important nutrient and antioxidant. But research on cats has shown that carotenoid pigments aren't normally found in their plasma or other tissues. The studies go on to report that felines require preformed vitamin A in their diet because they lack the ability to make the conversion from beta-carotene. This ingredient is an antioxidant, however, so maybe it's connected to the marketing claim on the package that states "Advanced Antioxidant Formula."

— **Minerals (potassium chloride, calcium sulfate, salt, ferrous sulfate, zinc oxide, copper sulfate, manganous oxide, calcium iodate, sodium selenite).** These are about half the number of well-known minerals, not including the many trace elements. The first one listed here is potassium chloride. Potassium is certainly an important mineral, but it's interesting to note that it's never found isolated in real foods; in nature, it's bound with other nutrients. Feline studies have shown that the level of potassium needed depends greatly on the quality and quantity of protein being consumed. For example, the more soy protein in the diet, the more of this mineral is required.

There have been no animal reproductive studies done for potassium chloride, but in humans it's not recommended for use during pregnancy because it may harm the unborn child. Also, in human studies, it's been found that potassium chloride shouldn't be used by individuals with kidney disease, Addison's disease, stomach problems, or diarrhea; and it shouldn't be taken in conjunction with certain medications. It may also cause allergic reactions.

Potassium chloride has a wide range of applications. In addition to supplying a source of potassium in processed food products, it's a food additive for stabilizing and thickening. It's also used to melt ice on winter roadways and as a fertilizer. Stanford University recommends euthanizing lab cats with an overdose of potassium chloride while under general anesthesia. The mineral is part of the lethal-injection cocktail given to death-row inmates as an overdose that causes a rapid increase in heart rate.

In appropriate doses, potassium chloride may be just fine, and it's found on store shelves as a supplement, but the amount used in cat-food products can vary greatly—and we have no way of knowing how much is in any particular batch. Even so, the form found in food is sounding better all the time.

You'll notice that two of the minerals in this part of the ingredient list have *calcium* in their names, but only the calcium sulfate is used as a source of this mineral (a poorly utilized, nonanimal form). You may also recognize this chemical combination as common blackboard chalk! The calcium iodate provides iodine; it's also used in dusting powders, lotions, ointments, and deodorants.

Another mineral, salt, isn't necessarily a bad thing, and since the label doesn't name the exact form, I'll assume it's sodium chloride—table salt. This contributes to hypertension and kidney and heart disease, and it induces thirst in cats.

Pet-food manufacturers have a choice as to what form of mineral supplements they use in their formulas. The sulfates and oxides are considered less desirable than other, more expensive forms because they're insoluble in water. Also, there may be many other chemicals added to the mineral powders used in manufacturing, and the synthetic versions can act quite differently in the body than natural-food forms. For example, ferrous sulfate is an inorganic form of iron that destroys vitamin E; organic iron doesn't have this harmful effect.

What's in the Bag?

— **Vitamins (choline chloride, vitamin A supplement, vitamin D_3 supplement, vitamin E supplement, ascorbic acid (a source of vitamin C), niacin, thiamine, calcium pantothenate, riboflavin, pyridoxine hydrochloride, folic acid, biotin, vitamin B_{12} supplement).** There are at least 16 well-known vitamins, and this product contains 13. I guess that's pretty close! It's odd that most of the B vitamins are listed by their chemical names—except for vitamin B_{12} supplement. Why isn't it listed as cyanocobalamin? Or, conversely, why isn't choline chloride listed as vitamin B_4? 'Tis a puzzlement!

Also, it would be preferable if they'd state the sources. For example, if you have a cat with an allergy to yeast, then you'd want to know if these B vitamins are derived from yeast. It's an inexpensive source, so it's very popular, but can cause health problems in the many animals that are sensitive to it.

Likewise, it's not very informative to simply list "vitamin E supplement" when there are many forms of this nutrient. Studies have shown the synthetic form to be much less effective and potentially harmful, while the natural form supports health. The same holds true for vitamin A. Which forms are they using here?

Evaluation

Personally, I wouldn't feel comfortable feeding my cat a product such as the one analyzed here or the many other processed pet foods like it. And remember, this one is sold in veterinarian offices, is more expensive than many others, and is considered a "premium" brand. But after thorough examination, I found that it contains poor-quality ingredients and many substances that aren't at all appropriate for the feline species. There are more nutrients in real food. My cat may not be able to fully meet its nutritional needs by eating this product. And if that's the case, my cat's body might not be strong enough to maintain optimal health.

This chapter has examined the ingredients on the label. Next we'll look at what the heat used in manufacturing processed pet-food products does to the ingredients and how that can affect feline health.

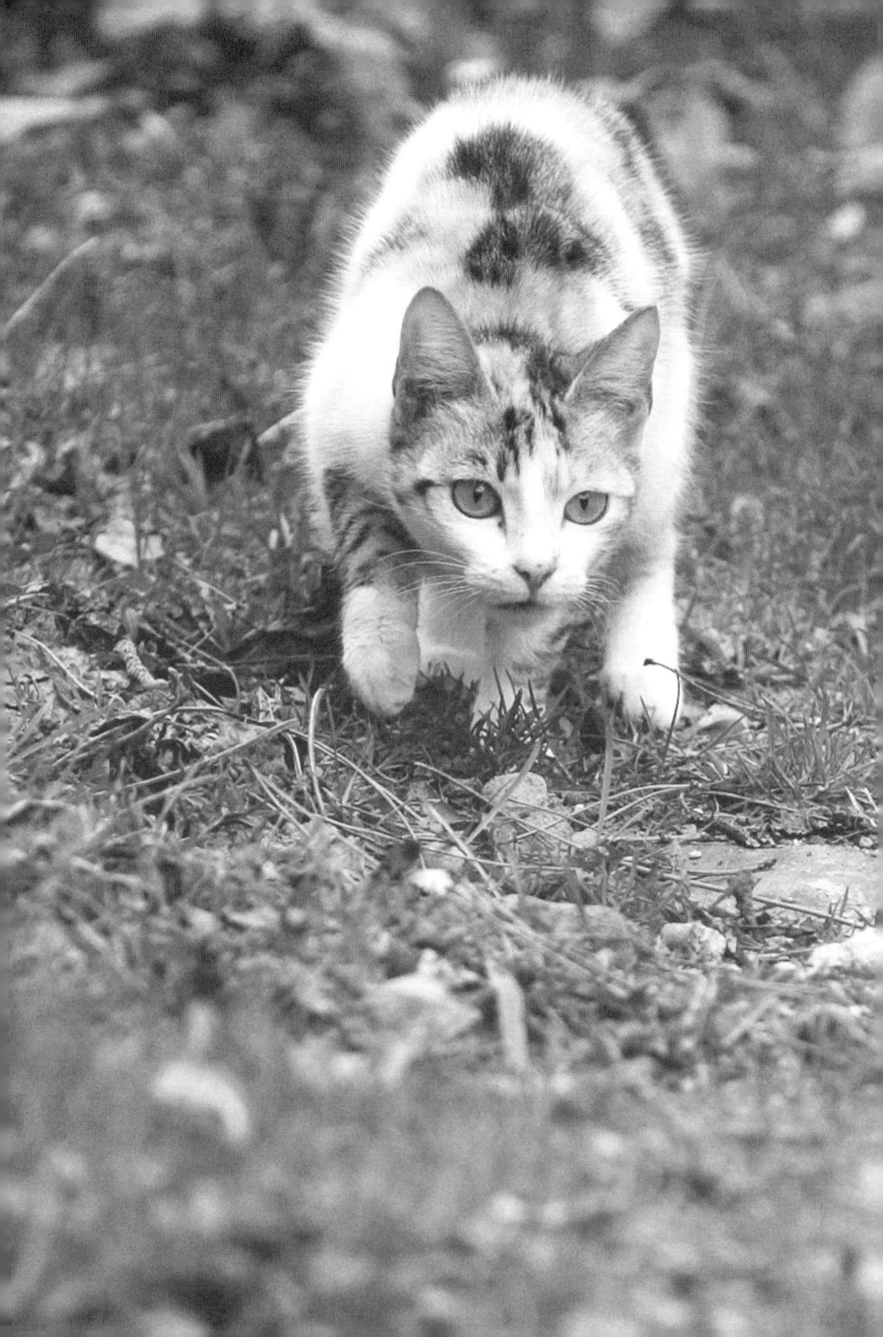

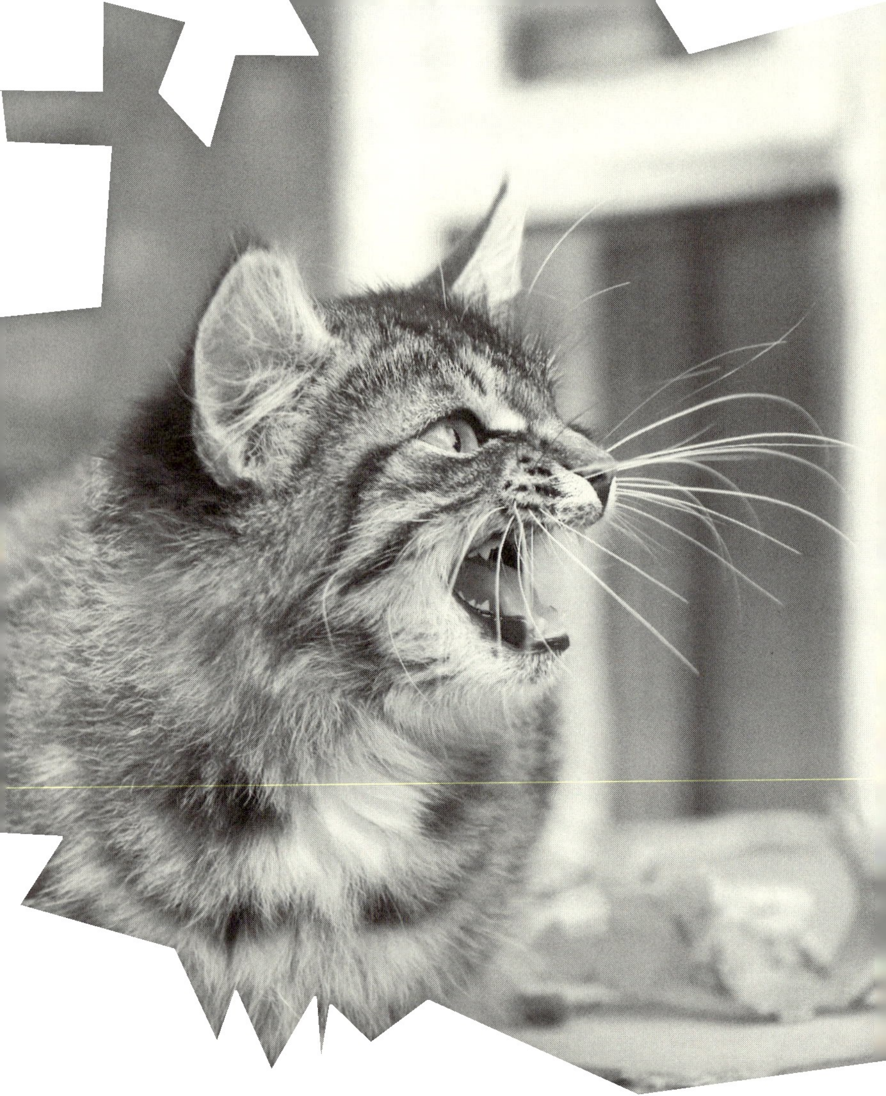

CHAPTER 7

Turning Up the Heat

*"Prowling his own quiet backyard or asleep by the fire,
he is still only a whisker away from the wilds."*
— Jean Burden

So what if I could take the product that disappointed me in Chapter 6 and make it better? Or what if I could develop my own processed petfood product with high-quality ingredients in the bag or can? Then would I feed it to my cat? Nope! It wouldn't fit into my comfort zone because these types of processed pet-food products are *cooked*. In fact, they're subjected to very high temperatures. Let's take a look now at what heat does to food and how that affects its ability to fulfill my cat's nutritional requirements.

— **Protein.** Research at the National Cancer Institute and John Hopkins University in the U.S. and the Queen Elizabeth Hospital in London, and other studies—including those conducted by experts in Japan and Europe—show that cooking meat with high temperatures creates chemicals that aren't present when it's raw. Seventeen different carcinogenic (cancer-causing) compounds develop that collectively are called heterocyclic amines (HCAs). These HCAs interfere with the body's genetic structure and are proven to cause cancer in animals. They're specifically linked to cancer of the stomach, pancreas, colon, heart, and breast. The substances are even found in nursing youngsters, so we know they travel through breast milk.

Other research shows that heat processing may have a very negative effect on the quality of protein and create unnatural amino-acid cross-linking. The Maillard reaction was named after the French scientist Louis-Camille Maillard, who discovered that sugars and amino acids react together when heated to form new chemicals. These are foreign substances not found in nature.

In addition to altering amino acids (the building blocks of protein), heat destroys many of them. That's one reason why taurine is put into cat-food products. The animal protein should provide it, but after heat processing, the nutrient is so diminished that it has to be added back in as a supplement.

But what about the other essential amino acids? The National Research Council quotes a study stating that there are ten amino acids essential for growing kittens, and if any of them aren't present, the animal will suffer. They also note that they don't know the minimal amino-acid requirements of adult cats for maintenance or for pregnancy and lactation. Using raw animal protein helps take the guesswork out of providing natural amino acids, as they haven't been destroyed by heat and are readily available for our cats' bodies to put to good use.

— **Fat.** We all know what happens to animal fat when it's heated: It turns into grease. Raw fat has so many important functions for cats, but when it's heated, it can't do good work in the body. It's unable to provide transportation for fat-soluble vitamins or the energy a feline body needs. Heat changes essential fatty acids into dangerous trans-fatty acids. Many studies have been done proving the connection between ingestion of trans fats and disease. For example, they interfere with insulin receptors and are linked to type 2 diabetes, cancer, infertility, heart disease, and more. You may have noticed that many human-food products in your grocery store now declare they're free of these substances due to the many studies proving their dangers. You should also know that fats and oils are easily damaged not only by heat, but also by light and oxygen.

— **Minerals and vitamins.** Heat destroys and/or alters almost all vitamins and minerals, which is one reason you see so many added back into pet-food products. If they were still there after the high-temperature processing, the manufacturer wouldn't need to reintroduce them. These nutrients are best utilized by the body in their natural food forms, and unfortunately, many that are put into pet-food products are synthetic, isolated versions. Another problem is that even when they're added to the products, they deteriorate rather quickly, so you really have no way of knowing if they're still viable by the time you use the product.

— **Grains.** Although they aren't a part of a cat's natural diet and shouldn't be fed to them, we'll take a look at what heat does to grain because it's such a large part of most pet-food products. In 2002, researchers in Sweden discovered that heating high-carbohydrate foods produces a chemical called acrylamide. Since that time, studies done in the U.S. and other countries have confirmed those findings. The Environmental Protection Agency classifies acrylamide as a probable carcinogen (Group B2). Animal studies show that it causes gene mutations, neurotoxic effects, and cancer—especially in the breast and uterus—along with tumors of the adrenal glands and scrotum.

More Problems

Heat processing changes the molecular structure of food and, as noted above, creates unfamiliar substances and interactions. It also decreases the water content, which is an important consideration in feline health since much of a cat's moisture intake should come from what it eats. This species doesn't naturally drink a lot of water because it's designed to consume raw food with its moisture content intact.

Heat also destroys all enzymes found in raw food. Food enzymes aid the digestion and utilization of nutrients. Without them, the cat's body has to produce more enzymes from its own reserves. This can place added stress on the pancreas and other organs. Raw foods—especially proteins and fats—are so much more easily digested that they only take about one-half to one-third the amount of time to pass through the digestive tract as cooked food.

Products subjected to heat can also contribute to obesity due to the fact that the body isn't getting all the nutrients it needs, so it may tend to compensate by overeating. Cooked protein and fat is more difficult to digest than the raw versions, so it uses up more energy. This is a drain on the body and affects health, activity, and longevity. Also, when digestion is impaired, it may not create some of the nutrients and biochemicals that are naturally formed in the body. For example, vitamin K and some of the B vitamins are actually produced within a healthy digestive system.

Raw-Food Studies

In 1930, Dr. Paul Kouchakoff of the Institute of Clinical Chemistry in Switzerland studied the effect of cooked and raw food on the immune system. He found that when cooked food is ingested, the blood responds by increasing the number of white blood cells. This phenomenon is called "digestive leukocytosis." Normally, an increase in leukocytes (white blood cells) happens as a defense mechanism for stress, infection, trauma, toxins, or anything harmful. Dr. Kouchakoff discovered raw food didn't cause this reaction. After much research, he concluded that raw food was viewed by the immune system as "friendly," and cooked food was viewed as dangerous. Because this reaction negatively affects the entire body, he called the overall effect "pathological leukocytosis."

In the 1930 and '40s, Dr. Francis Pottenger proved the importance of feeding raw food (based on raw meat) to cats with his now-famous study. His research involved 900 felines over a ten-year period. The cats in the study were housed in outdoor enclosures and split into groups receiving cooked food, raw food, or a combination of both. He found that the cats on the entirely raw-food diet were very healthy and didn't need veterinary care, but the more the food was cooked, the less healthy the cats were. Over a period of three generations, the cats on the cooked diet continued to deteriorate in health until they could no longer reproduce normally.

Some interesting specifics of the cats eating cooked meat include a loss of bone density and problems with the heart, eyes, thyroid, kidneys, respiratory system, teeth, and gums. They developed arthritis, allergies, parasite infestations, and behavior problems. They also had intestinal tracts measuring 72 to 80 inches in length that lacked good tone and elasticity. Compare this to the healthy raw-meat cats that had an average intestinal length of only 48 inches with good tone and elasticity. Also, the raw-food cats had two to three times as much calcium and phosphorus in their bones.

I have a video of the actual Pottenger cat study that I used to show in my nutrition lectures, but I had to stop showing it because it was just too heartbreaking for most people to see the suffering of the cooked-food cats. It's ironic, really, how all these years later, many cat lovers are actually still repeating this research by feeding cooked pet-food products to their cats. And not surprisingly, many are seeing the same ill-health effects that Dr. Pottenger saw in his cooked-food cats. These people certainly don't intend to hurt their animal friends, it's just that the cooked-product companies are very large, powerful, and convincing in their marketing. So who's to blame for our cats' health problems? Let's take a closer look at that sensitive subject in the next chapter.

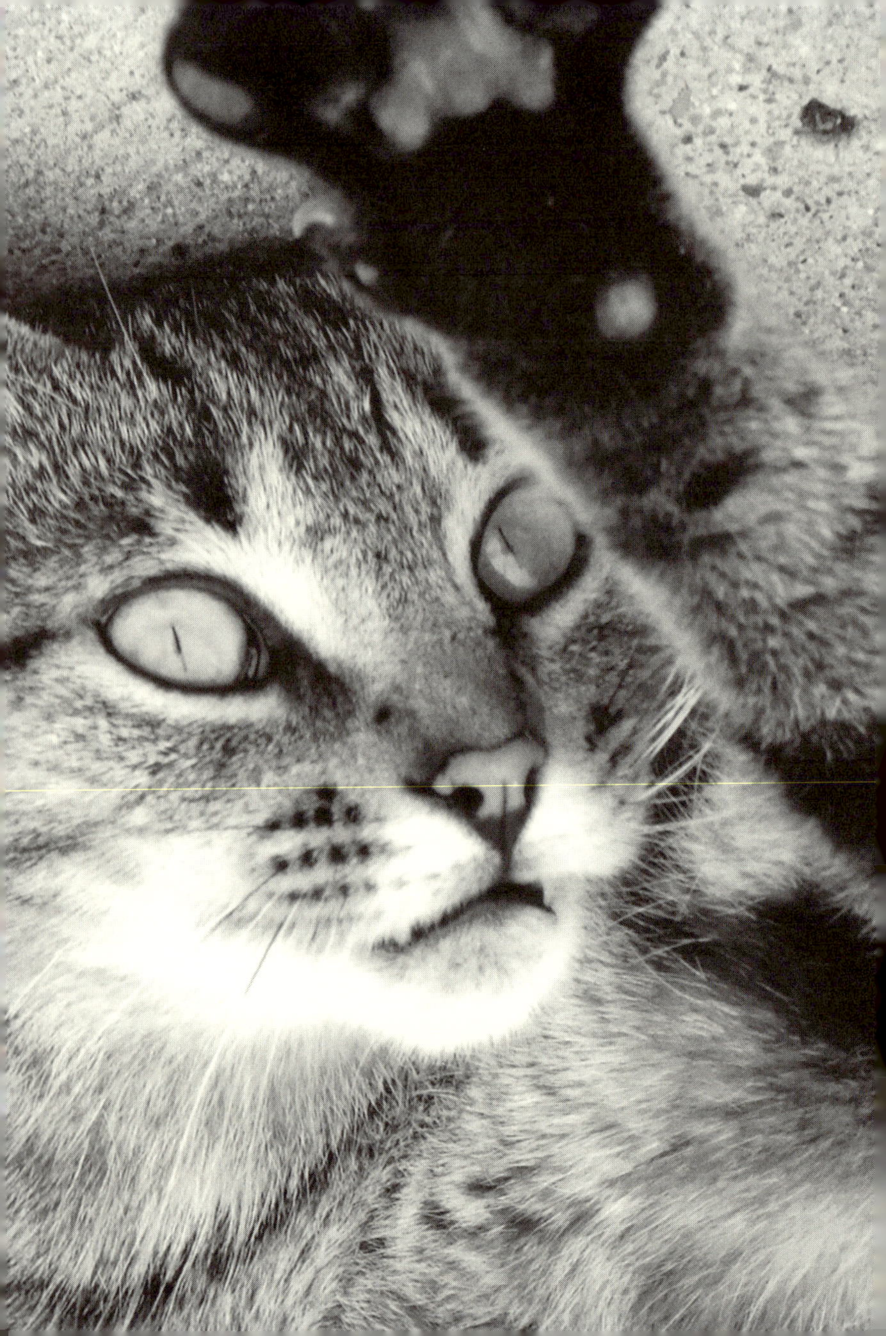

CHAPTER 8

Responsibility

*"Everything I know I learned from my cat:
When you're hungry eat. When you're tired,
nap in a sunbeam. When you go to
the vet's, pee on your owner."*
— Gary Smith

At this point in my investigative journey to decide what to feed my cats, the commercial, processed pet-food products were definitely not coming up roses—or even catnip. But let me state for the record that I *don't* think the manufacturers are purposely trying to harm our cats. I don't think there's a cigar-smoking executive sitting behind his desk (in a corner office with a big view window) doing a Snidely Whiplash impression while chanting: "I'm going to hurt some kitties today," followed by evil laughter, of course. No, it's not that personal—it's just business. It's like any other industry that makes billions of dollars every year: The bottom line is the top dollar.

I'm not faulting these companies for trying to make lots of money, but I don't have to approve of the way they do it. I'm certainly not a fan of animal testing, low-quality ingredients, components that aren't even appropriate for felines, too-frequent recalls, and questionable marketing tactics. But hey, when it comes down to it, my cat's health isn't really their responsibility.

Is my cat's health my veterinarian's responsibility? Not really. Yes, I go to vets for their professional opinions, which are very important to me. I respect their experience and education in most areas of animal health. But unless they've taken it upon themselves to study animal nutrition in an unbiased forum, they may not be the best source of advice for species-appropriate food for my cats. At veterinary schools, they receive very little education on this subject, and what they do get is mostly taught by employees of the larger pet-food companies. The little time devoted to nutrition usually involves the incomplete research we discussed earlier and heavy product pushing—not information about real *food.*

I have very dear friends who are veterinarians. Through their wisdom and my own experience and research, I've come to understand better why vets aren't always the best source of unbiased nutritional information. You see, when I was studying animal nutrition at Cornell University's College of Veterinary Medicine a few years ago, only a couple of my professors weren't paid employees of pet-food companies.

I'll never forget one particular lecture where the teacher/veterinarian was discussing the different forms of pet-food products—dry, canned, and so on. While she was talking about the semi-moist products, she mentioned in an offhand way that she would never feed them to *her* pets. Then she quickly laughed and said, "Oh, my boss would kill me if he heard me say that!"

I didn't find it amusing. It was painfully clear that she was repeating (except for her slipup) what the pet-food company wanted the students to hear—not unbiased information or her actual opinion.

The biggest pet-food companies hire brilliant marketers to sell their products. After all, what could be better than having experts (veterinarians) endorse your product? How did this come about? Well, one of the parent companies that's become very involved with vets also makes toothpaste. Do you remember the old advertisement that boasted eight out of ten dentists recommend a particular brand? It was a brilliant campaign and put this firm at the top of toothpaste sales.

At the time, the company also had a very small pet-food division they were about to sell, but an executive came forward with a great idea: If they could use the same tactic with this branch as they had with their toothpaste, they'd be equally successful. So they used the pharmaceutical industry's practice of spending tons of money to woo doctors. In fact, a retired sales executive from the pet-food company commented on why this marketing strategy works so well: "It's just like taking drugs: You go to the doctor, and he prescribes something for you, and you don't much question what the doctor says. It's the same with animals."

They know that the trust cat guardians have in vets is so strong that they'll feed what they're told without question. So the manufacturer spends a great deal of money enforcing that connection. In fact, other than universities, this company is the country's largest employer of vets! They fund research and nutrition courses and professorships at veterinary colleges and offer a formal nutrition-certification program for technicians. They've also written a widely used textbook on animal nutrition that's given free of charge to veterinary students, who also receive stipends and get products at zero or almost-zero charge.

This relationship doesn't end after graduation. The corporation sends veterinarians to seminars on how to better sell their products, provides sales-goal-oriented promotions, gives them lots of promotional tools, and offers big discounts so that vets make more money on product sales.

There's really no point in naming names in this situation because these practices aren't confined to a single pet-food company. Although one or two used to have a corner on the veterinary market, others have now reaped the rewards of employing similar strategies. It's genius, really, and I can understand that many veterinarians have busy practices and may feel that they don't have time to investigate pet foods more closely. It certainly must be easier and less time-consuming to simply suggest a familiar product and be done with it, but if they've got such an extremely close association with a pet-food company, we may reasonably assume that it might be difficult for them to offer an unbiased opinion on nutrition to their clients.

Please understand that there are more and more vets today who *are* taking the time to learn about real-food nutrition. And with their busy schedules, I truly respect the ones who do; and I like to support these independent, open-minded individuals who enjoy continuing their education.

The bottom line is that my cat's health is *my* responsibility, and your cat's health is *your* responsibility. We choose which veterinarian to take our cats to. We choose to follow our vets' advice or not. We choose which type of food to feed our cats. All the choices are up to us, so choose wisely, grasshopper (my cats love to eat those guys)!

I *won't* be feeding grasshoppers, but in the next chapter I'll talk about preparing homemade meals for cats. Okay, maybe one grasshopper for dessert—but the cat has to catch it because I'm not touching it!

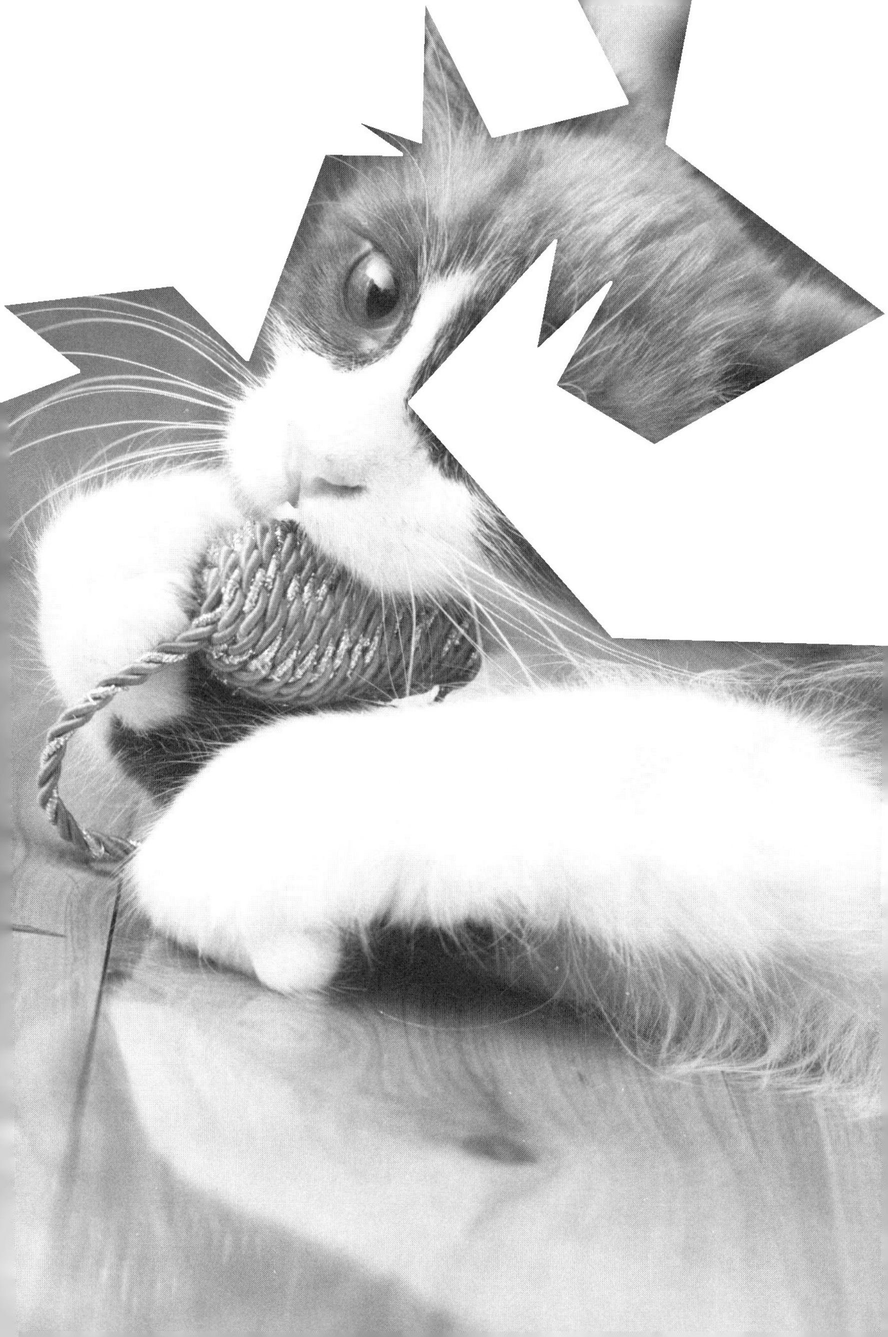

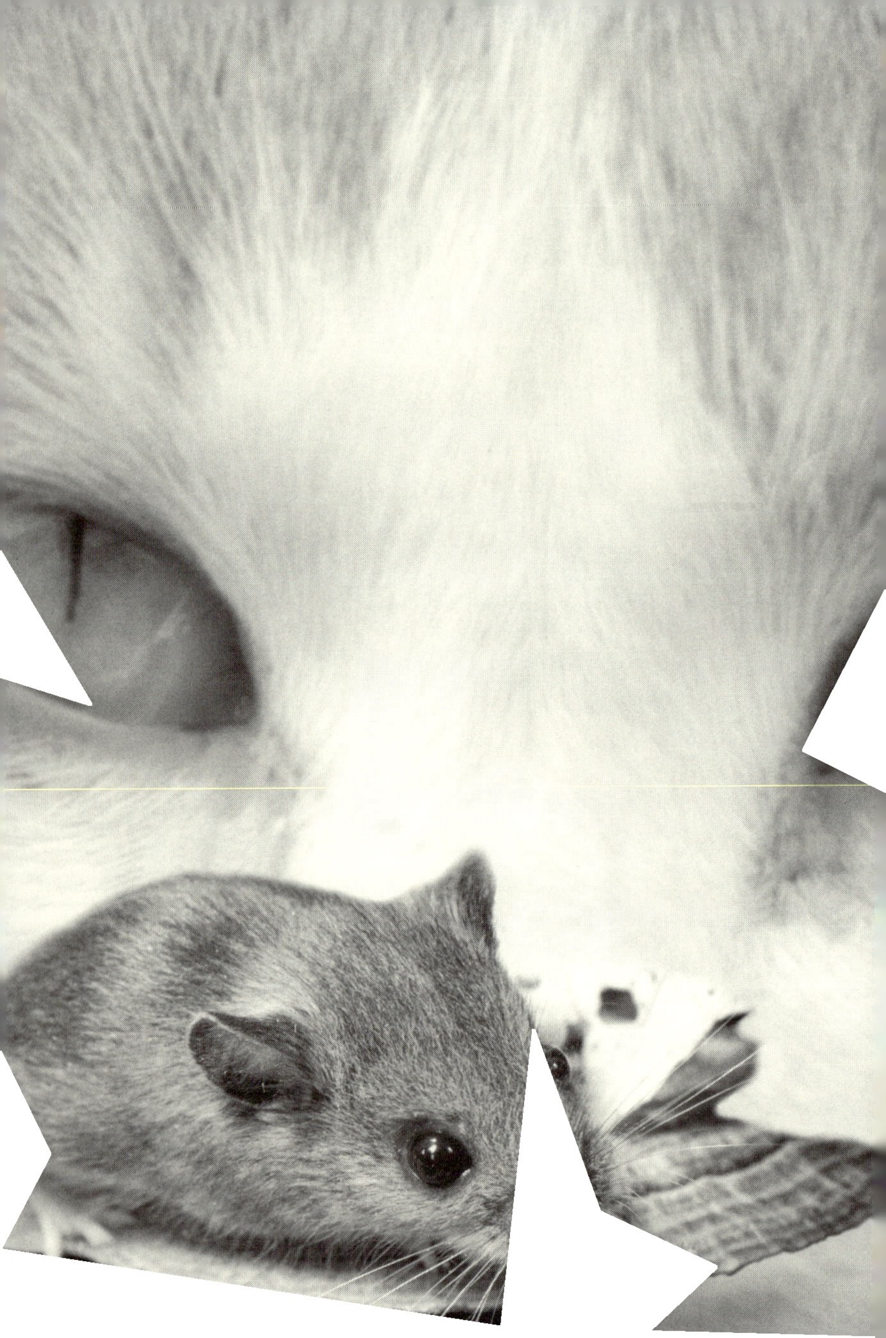

CHAPTER 9

To Boldly Go Where Millions Have Gone Before

"Love to eat them mousies . . . mousies what I love to eat! Bite they little heads off, nibble on they tiny feet."
— B. Kliban

After doing the research, I felt that I could make a more nutritious meal for my cats at home than could be provided by a commercial product. Making pet food is certainly not a new "fad." In fact, it's been done for many thousands of years—longer than anyone has had "store-bought" options! Think about it—those cans and bags have really only been around for a very short period of time. For thousands of years before they were invented, humans managed to provide cats with healthy meals just fine. And of course, many outdoor felines "dined out" on their own.

There's no proof that feeding your cats a processed pet food is better for them than a properly prepared meal of fresh, species-appropriate food. And anyone who says cats are living longer today *because* of those processed products also has no proof. Certainly, a cat may live longer today if it's not outside being hit by a car or attacked by another predator. But the cats of my grandmother's day were frequently living well into their late 20s without benefit of processed products. Feeding real food is really just the longest used way of feeding cats. And since I've been doing this for about two decades, I'm pleased to be carrying on the tradition. But I'm far from the only one witnessing a resurgence of feline health due to this method. As more people make the switch to feeding their cats species-appropriate real food, we're seeing cats live the long, healthy lives they were meant to live.

And here's more good news: Making a nutritious meal for your cat is easy. I find it much easier than preparing meals for myself or my human family! Don't let anyone convince you that you're not capable of feeding your cat real food. If you manage to feed yourself and live—and I assume you're still alive since you're reading this book—then you can provide for your cat. Personally, I find it insulting for anyone to imply that we're not intelligent enough to feed our own cats, that it's too difficult for us and so we must use a commercial product. If cat lovers were incapable of this simple task, the "domestic" feline would have become extinct many years ago!

I'd like to bring up an additional point about the bizarre opinion that you must feed your cat only commercial pet-food products, with this question; this may sound silly at first, but I really want you to consider it seriously: Would *you* eat dry or canned cat food? Would you consume it exclusively, day in and day out, for your entire life? Would you give it to your human children every day for their entire lives? Remember, nothing else can be eaten, just this one product. Now stop giggling, I'm trying to make a point here!

Your answer was probably a resounding: "No, yuck!" And why do you feel this way? Your first thought may have been the gross-out factor. After that, you might have realized that if someone said that you (and your family) must *only* eat a heavily processed dry- or canned-food product for humans and *nothing* else, no fresh food *ever,* you'd probably think they didn't know what they were talking about. After all, experts are telling us every day to eat *fewer* processed food products and more fresh food if we wish to enjoy good health and longevity. They tell us that unprocessed food contains important nutrients missing from processed products, which may also contain substances that can actually harm us. The same basic nutritional sense applies to our feline friends.

If using commercial pet food has become a habit for you, then it may take just a little brain "rebooting" to change your routine. Personally, after I first decided that I wanted to make my own cat food, I freaked out a little. What helped me most was plain old common sense and logic. I realized there really wasn't any reason to believe that a processed product could supply a more nutritious meal for my cat than I could.

I had to shake that marketing out of my head. I'd read the labels and ingredients on those cans and bags, and I knew I could definitely do better! By using a cat's natural diet as my guide, I could make meals that would provide feline-appropriate nutrients. Unlike the pet-food companies, the nutrition would come from fresh, raw foods, so I wouldn't have to guess what nutrients had been destroyed or altered during heat and processing like manufacturers do. And my ingredients would definitely be "fit for human consumption," unlike most pet-food products.

One thing did bother me at first: How was I going to feed the correct "percentages" of ingredients? You know—the labels on the bags and cans say that they contain a certain percent of protein, fat, and so on. Math was never my strong point, so how was I going to figure it out? Then that good old common sense and logic I mentioned earlier came to my rescue, and I did find the solution. Percentage-wise, the lion's share (pun intended) would be muscle and organ meat, and next would be bone, which is very important, also.

I remembered that just because percentages were listed on the product label didn't mean they were correct for my cat anyway. After all, the protein analysis was determined by a combination of a little bit of animal protein and a lot of grain. Because we often think that protein equals meat, we might assume that a label declaring 40 percent protein derives that figure from *animal* ingredients, but as we saw in the earlier product-label deconstruction, it may include a lot of nonanimal, incomplete, and totally inappropriate vegetable components.

It also struck me that eating according to percentages was very odd and certainly not something we do for ourselves. Of course, we should have an idea of the correct foods and the general proportions to use, and I'll share these later, but eating according to strict percentages isn't the norm. We don't compose our meals or our children's that way. I don't go into a restaurant and say, "Yes, waiter, I'll have 30 percent protein, 20 percent fat, 10 percent moisture . . ." and so on. And I'm pretty sure that when a cat catches a mouse, it doesn't ask itself if the mouse has the correct "percentage" of each ingredient before devouring it.

The best way to get the "percentage" thing correct is to keep the cat's natural dietary needs in mind. It's easier if you forget numbers and think proper ingredients and proportions instead. If you can't visualize that, visit a pet store that has mice, rats, rabbits, birds, fish, and reptiles. Take a good look at them because they have the correct ingredients and proportions. We'll keep those critters in mind while preparing well-balanced, easy-to-make meals of nutritious ordinary foods in our home kitchens. And although your cats may wish that you'd brought home dinner from that pet store (feline take-out?), they'll also greatly benefit from your homemade kitty cuisine!

The C.A.T. Diet

When people ask what food I recommend for cats, I say "The C.A.T. diet, of course!" The letters stand for Cat-Appropriate and Tasty. It's a raw diet using foods that provide felines with the nutrients they need to be healthy and happy. We'll lay the groundwork in this chapter, and then in Chapter 14 you'll find specific recipes for your feline friend. If you're wondering why I recommend a raw diet for cats, please reread the chapter on what heat does to food and nutrients.

Because our goal is to make meals that our cats can easily digest and utilize, we'll use foods that are as close as we can get to what a cat might eat in nature. We'll keep in mind the carnivorous structure of its body, inside and out, when we make and serve our meals. We'll also be realistic, putting together dishes with readily available ingredients that will fulfill feline nutritional needs. This chapter discusses the ingredients we'll use and gives a bit of information about them.

Muscle Meat

This is found between the skin and bone—for example, a chicken breast, leg, or thigh is muscle meat. Good options for felines include chicken, turkey, Cornish game hens, quail, guinea fowl, and rabbit. Of course, there are other meat animals you can use, but these particular ones are easy for most cats to digest, especially as they transition to their new diet. But be ready to experiment with a variety to discover your cat's favorites. After all, in nature the cat wouldn't just eat mice, but perhaps birds, reptiles, and insects as well. Variety is the spice of life! By the way, dark meat is often more nutritious, and it contains more taurine than white meat.

Since the jury is out on the safety of feeding raw pork, you'll probably want to avoid it. Small fish such as smelt, grunion, and sardines can be given occasionally. In my area, there's a smelt "season," and these little fish can be bought fresh and cheap—just how I like 'em! Fish today often contain heavy metals and other toxins, and the higher up a fish is on the food chain, the more toxins it has. That's why the smaller ones are better choices. It's probably a good idea to offer fish no more than once a week anyway, since feeding it more often may cause other nutrient deficiencies. And never feed raw salmon, as it may cause a disease called, aptly enough, salmon poisoning.

Chicken, Cornish game hen, and turkey are some of the least expensive and easiest meats to find at your local butcher or grocery store, but remember to introduce a variety of meats once your cat is readily eating their new diet.

Raw Meat and Bacteria

Okay, let's discuss the obvious—raw meat and bacteria. First, raw meat does not automatically contain negative bacteria. Plus, we should remember that cats have been eating raw meat for many thousands of years. Your cat may be eating raw food right now! If they occasionally dine on rodents, birds, reptiles, bugs, or the like, they're eating some raw food already. Obviously, their bodies are designed to thrive on it, or their species would have died out long ago.

The feline digestive system hasn't changed. It's still short and acidic, which is great for eating raw meat that may have some negative bacteria. It's a brilliant design: Eat the food, digest it, and get the waste out quickly. It doesn't give germs much time to set up house. This is a very different design from a cow, for example. If a cow ate raw meat, it would be in their lengthy digestive system for so long that it would putrefy, setting up a great environment for harmful bacteria to multiply. Cows are designed to be herbivores, but cats are still obligatory carnivores that must eat meat to survive.

Another plus is that raw meat is undamaged by heat. Its amino acids—including the all-important taurine and other nutrients—are intact and easy to utilize. In fact, the enzymes that raw meat contains (but cooked meat doesn't) aid in its digestion. It also provides the essential fatty acids that a cat must get from an animal source.

There's no proof that a properly prepared raw-food diet is harmful. If a veterinarian tells you that it will make your cat sick, ask him how many cats with health problems he sees per month—probably quite a few. Considering that the majority of his clients are likely to be feeding their cats a high-heat processed pet food, it's logical to conclude that eating those products is certainly no safer or more health promoting than a good raw diet. And what about all those recalls? Commercial cat foods contribute to health problems and deaths every year.

If you go to a veterinarian who promotes raw-food diets—and their numbers are growing every day—he'll tell you that he rarely, if ever, sees problems related to raw meat contamination. In fact, he'll probably say that what he does see is a dramatic increase in health, just like the rest of us who have been doing this for years.

Please don't misunderstand—I fully acknowledge that it's possible for raw meat to contain bacteria such as E. coli or the like, and it's possible (but not common) for an individual to be affected by it. I just want to put the threat into perspective. One thing to remember is that negative bacteria are on many different things that you and your cat come into contact with every day. In fact, according to the Centers for Disease Control and Prevention, you have a greater change of getting E. coli from alfalfa sprouts, person-to-person contact, or a child's wading pool than you do from raw meat. So get your cat out of the pool!

Seriously, though, if you were to culture your cat's stool right now, you'd hopefully find a certain amount of E. coli because it's a normal inhabitant of your cat's gut. Here's what highly regarded Meridian Valley Laboratory has to say about it: "E. coli is the most common of the normal flora and is necessary for the proper digestion of foods and maintaining the proper balance of intestinal flora."

As for salmonella bacteria, the University of Colorado Health Sciences Center in Denver reports that it doesn't pose a threat to healthy animals. It's when an abnormal overgrowth of negative bacteria occurs that a body may suffer. This may be caused by many factors, including a lack of good gut flora, antibiotics, and other drugs. I'm not advising you to refuse these drugs if they're needed, but it's probably a good idea to supplement your cat's digestive system with nondairy probiotics (good bacteria) to rebuild a healthy internal environment.

Probiotics are microorganisms that improve the intestinal tract's microbial balance. There are many strains, but you may recognize one of the most popular as lactobacillus acidophilus. When purchasing a probiotic product, look for one that states it's nondairy and contains multibillions of viable organisms. Personally, I'd avoid those that contain FOS, which is a prebiotic that's meant to help feed the probiotic. Many are sugars, however, that I've found cats don't tolerate well. Of course, check the label to make sure the product doesn't contain any other added fillers or such that you don't want to give your cat.

Experts report that antibiotics, which destroy both good and bad bacteria, may affect intestinal balance for up to a year after they've been discontinued. Nondairy probiotics can be used anytime you want to boost the population of "good guys" in the gastrointestinal system that help keep the "bad guys" under control. They're reported to help cats pass hair balls more easily as well and may help your cat more easily transition to its new diet.

More about Raw Meat

I've discovered that in some cases the acceptance of a diet that includes raw meat can be connected to cultural preferences and tradition. I once taught a class on animal nutrition to a group of Japanese veterinary students, and they had absolutely no hesitation in accepting the fact that raw animal protein is good for cats. After all, they've been eating it themselves all their lives with good results! Every culture has traditional raw meat or fish dishes. In fact, the very best high-class restaurants in the U.S. get top dollar for uncooked dishes such as steak tartare or sushi. That reminds me—if you're like me and love sushi and sashimi, have you ever noticed the "buzz" of energy you get or how good you feel after eating it? I sure do. That raw protein does my body good!

To further assure that we don't encourage contamination in our cats' food, we'll use human-grade meat and practice the same sanitary habits that we do when preparing meals for our human family. We'll wash everything the meat touches, including our hands, utensils, countertops, and dishes. We'll store the meat in the refrigerator or freezer, defrost it properly, and use it before the expiration date—good old common sense. And please use that same common sense if you feel that your cat shouldn't eat raw meat for some medical reason. While many nutritionally oriented vets feel that such a diet helps cats with compromised immune systems, a few prefer to feed cooked meat to these animals, at least for a little while. Every cat is an individual.

The form of raw meat you feed depends on you and your cat. Whole pieces or chunks are best because they require the same tearing action that a prey animal would, and that's great exercise and stimulation. But if you or your cat prefer, you can use ground meat. An important reminder is to never feed your cat an all-meat diet. That wouldn't be good since many nutrients would be missing. Remember, there are no hamburger patties or turkey cutlets running around outside! When a cat catches and eats a prey animal, it's consuming more than just muscle meat. As an ingredient in the C.A.T. diet, however, muscle meat offers important nutrients such as essential amino acids, vitamins, minerals, and essential fatty acids.

Organ Meat

Yep, organ meat means ooey-gooey gopher guts! Okay, I'm kidding, unless you find a gopher farm that can supply you with them. Preferably, you'll use organ meat from the same type of animal as the muscle meat in a particular meal. So, if you're working with chicken muscle, you'll use chicken organ meat. If you prepare something that doesn't match up this way, it's not the end of the world—just aim for the same as often as possible.

This ingredient is just what it sounds like: the organs of an animal, such as the liver, kidneys, and so on. The heart, although a unique muscle, is often considered part of this category; and it's especially important to include it in cat meals due to its high taurine content. Isn't it nifty that the nutrients in raw heart help prevent heart problems?

Organ meats are nutrient dense, but you don't want to use them exclusively because they're very rich, high in phosphorus, and low in calcium.

They are an integral part of the feline diet, however, offering amino acids, B vitamins, zinc, manganese, essential fatty acids, and much more. After all, a cat wouldn't catch and eat a mouse that was missing its liver or heart!

A note about a unique and wonderful food called green tripe: This is the stomach lining, and it's loaded with enzymes and good nutrients. Only feed *green* tripe, not the bleached white stuff at the grocery store. For variety, it can be used on its own as a complete meal. You can tell someone is a true animal lover if they're feeding this to their cats because it's very stinky. When I open a package, I get an installment of "Cats Gone Wild" because they love the stuff so much!

Bone

Okay, I'd like to see a show of hands—who knows where cats would find calcium in their natural diet? Yes, you're correct: They'd eat the bones of their prey. Of course, these would be raw, too, because cats don't set up campfires to roast their dinner. And it's a good thing they don't, because *cooked* bones can be very dangerous; they're quite brittle, dry, and sharp.

Raw bone has all sorts of necessary nutrients for cats such as vitamins, minerals, and enzymes. It also contains nutrient-rich marrow, collagen, and cartilage and is a good source of chondroitin. These last ingredients are often put in high-priced supplements for arthritis sufferers. And unfortunately, these days we can add cats to that group.

At my house, we call chicken necks "cat candy" because the kitties go crazy over them. As a bonus, they're also a good source of taurine. Whole bones are definitely most felines' favorite part of the meal. If you're not comfortable offering this ingredient in big pieces, they can be smashed or ground. You can get a good mix of meat and bone by grinding up a whole fryer (chicken) or the like, such as rabbit if that's on the menu. If you do so, all you need to add is organ meat and perhaps a couple of supplements (we'll cover these in the recipes), and you're good to go.

I know people who have their butchers grind up whole chickens or turkeys for them, and other folks own grinders and do it themselves. Keep in mind that ground really isn't as good as whole, and your cats will miss the fun, exercise, and stimulation of crunching on the intact bone, but they'll still get nutritional benefits. Whatever works best for you is fine, however, because it still beats a processed pet food.

I'm not a big fan of bonemeal because it's a high-heat processed product that may contain heavy metals and other toxins. It simply can't offer the same nutritional benefits as the real thing. If bones are the only thing holding you back from feeding a raw diet, using bonemeal with the other species-appropriate ingredients can still make a better meal than a commercial product. But before you go this route, consider finely grinding real bones if that fits into your comfort zone. You can do this yourself or you can have someone do it for you.

Supplements

If your cat is eating real, whole, fresh prey animals such as an entire mouse with everything intact, you probably don't need to add anything else to its diet. Face it, a fresh field mouse that's spent its life dining on *its* natural diet would provide your cat with everything it needs. And this is actually a good way to feed your house carnivore if you can do it. Mice and chicks are raised for reptile food, and most folks have no qualms about giving those animals their natural diet. But I realize that many people don't want to feed their cats this way. So if you're not feeding prey animals to your cat but rather preparing their meals in your kitchen, there are a couple of extras you may want to add.

— **Essential Fatty Acids.** The first is an essential fatty acid supplement containing fish-body oil and perhaps a little evening-primrose or borage oil. Note that fish *body* oil is a different product than fish *liver* oil. Fish or cod-liver oil is a great EFA supplement if you need the additional vitamins A and D that it contains, but your cat will be getting those from the raw liver in the recommended recipes. If you've omitted the raw liver for some reason (which I don't recommend), you may want to add a drop or two of cod-liver oil in its place.

The recommended essential fatty acids will help improve the ratios found in the domestic meat animals you'll be using and provide extra health benefits. Although, if you're only feeding grass-fed and finished meat you probably don't need to add EFAs because the ratios in the meat will be much better than that of animals raised conventionally on grain. Plus, here's a warning just to err on the side of caution: Studies with schizophrenic human patients taking phenothiazine epileptogenic drugs suggest that GLA oils such as evening primrose and borage shouldn't be used with these individuals. So to play it safe, if your cat has epilepsy, you may want to skip the GLA oils or at least discuss them with a qualified practitioner first. Otherwise, studies show these ingredients to be very helpful with some feline health issues.

— **Super Supp.** This is a special formula of mine (the recipe appears later in this book). I'd recommend starting with just a bit of it in your cat's food, working up to the recommended amount in the upcoming meal recipes. All of my cats obtain even greater vitality with this combination supplement in their diet. It combines a few ingredients that make up for nutrient depletion of our soils (and thus, our foods), modern-day stress, environmental toxins, and the extra nutrients that may be found in the cat's natural wild diet. I call it "Super Supp" for easy reference.

There are four basic ingredients: ground raw sunflower seeds, kelp or dulse powder, gelatin, and a very small amount of vitamin C. We'll mix these together in a jar, keeping meal preparation as simple as possible.

We'll use the seeds and kelp or dulse in a broken-down, pulverized form which is more suitable for our cats. These two ingredients are a powerful combination of nutrients. Ground, raw, shelled sunflower seeds offer too many nutrients to list here but include vitamin E, B vitamins, selenium, and manganese, among many others.

Kelp and dulse contain an immense array of nutrients, including calcium, iodine, B vitamins, and natural vitamin K, plus they help pull toxins from the body and have antibiotic activity. If your cat is hyperthyroid and you wish to avoid iodine, you could use organic spirulina (check that it's tested free of toxins) instead of kelp or dulse. The ground seeds and the kelp/dulse will also provide just a little bit of soluble and insoluble fiber in our cats' meals. Felines shouldn't have much fiber in their diets, so in this case, more isn't better.

Gelatin is a mixture of proteins extracted from animal collagen. It's often used for bone and joint health and as a digestive aid, and it's a good source of amino acids including L-proline, L-hydroxyproline, and glycine.

These are the major components of the supplement, but we'll also add a very small amount of buffered vitamin-C powder (such as calcium ascorbate) to act as an antioxidant and help protect the other ingredients from damage. Even though cats (unlike humans) make vitamin C within their bodies, many experts agree that they can benefit from additional supplementation. The *Norwegian Veterinary Journal* reports the assumption that animals are capable of producing sufficient quantities of vitamin C at all times is probably not valid and that under circumstances such as infection, trauma, or stress (physical or mental), larger amounts of the nutrient are needed by various tissues. Under these conditions, it's very possible that the animal's own production may not be able to keep up with demand.

Vitamin C helps strengthen the immune system and collagen; it's a natural anti-inflammatory, antihistamine, and antioxidant. The small amount of calcium in calcium ascorbate acts as a buffer, making it more stomach friendly, and it has a neutral pH. Our cats will only be getting a very small amount because it's only a small percent of the supplement, although some practitioners do use vitamin C in larger amounts medicinally. If you wish to investigate this, check the Internet and book suppliers. I feel that even though this supplement contains many important nutrients, it's best given to cats in small amounts.

Summary

So there you have it: The C.A.T. diet—Cat-Appropriate and Tasty! It's a simple combination of raw meat (muscle and organ), bone, and a few supplements (or "supps" as we call them at my house). The ingredients provide every known nutrient, and the meal is easy to prepare. In upcoming chapters, we'll talk about shopping for supplies, preparing the meal, recipes, and transitioning Mr. or Ms. Cat to the healthy new diet.

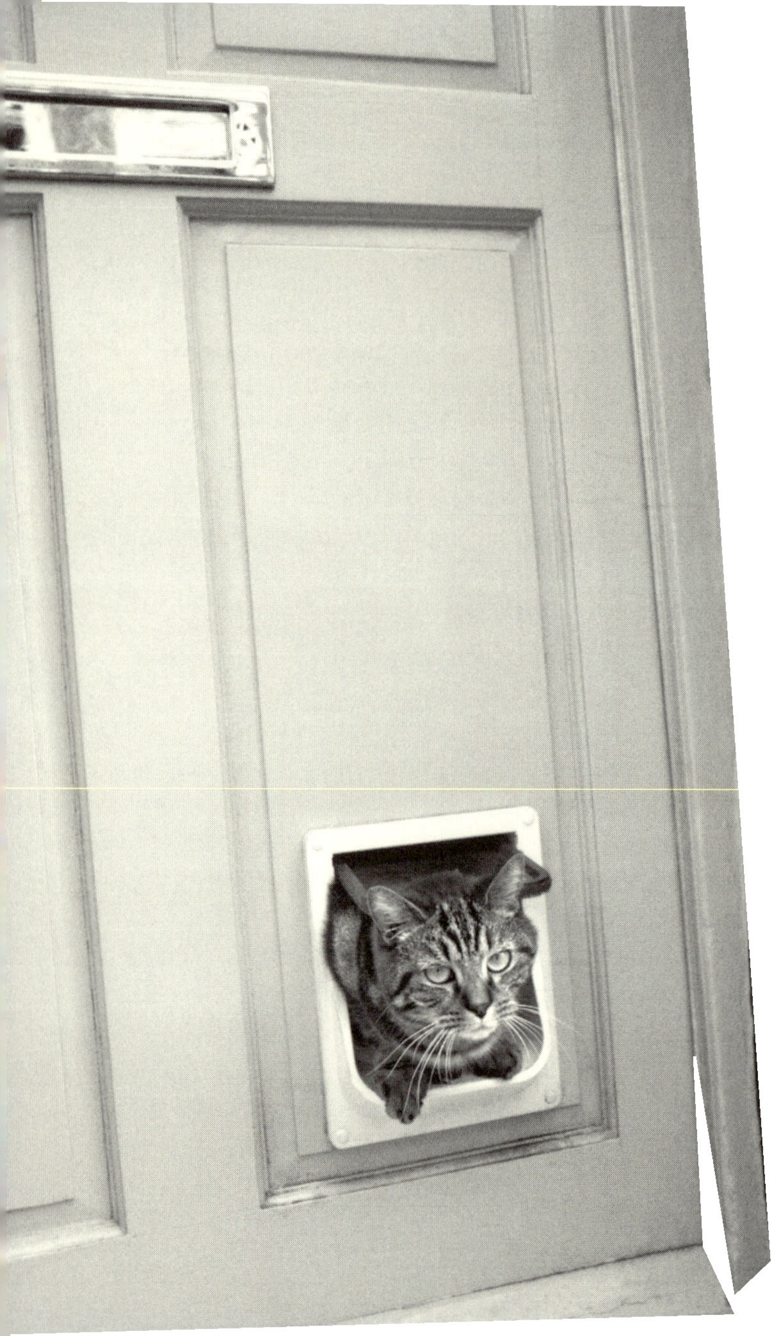

CHAPTER 10

Let's Go Shopping!

*"There is no snooze button on a cat
who wants breakfast."*
— Unknown

Shopping for the ingredients of the C.A.T. diet can be as easy as going to the store for your human family. It all depends on what sort of shopper you are and how you're going to be feeding the diet. For example, if you're going to have parts ground, you'll need to find a butcher to do that for you, or you'll have to purchase a grinder. If you're buying meat already ground or getting whole pieces, you don't have to do this. Once you put your mind to it, you'll find everything you need. My family has lived in quite a few different places over the years, and I've always been able to find the ingredients I need to make the cats' meals. Here's your shopping list:

The Meat of the Matter

1. Muscle meat
2. Organ meat (especially hearts and liver)
3. Bones (such as chicken necks, unless you're feeding whole animals or pieces containing bone)
4. Fish-body oil, plus evening-primrose oil or borage oil

The Super Supp

5. Raw, shelled sunflower seeds
6. Dulse or kelp powder
7. Plain gelatin powder
8. Calcium ascorbate powder

You'll be combining those last four ingredients and using only a small amount of each, so you probably won't need to purchase them often. Following are some buying tips for each ingredient:

1. Muscle meat. You have a few options here, so it all depends on what you're comfortable with. You can purchase ground meat (such as the ground chicken or turkey that comes in one-pound tubes or a package of any weight); whole pieces (such as thighs, breast, or legs, but go for the more nutritious dark meat when possible); or an entire bird or animal. An important tip from my experience is to talk to the people in charge of the meat department and tell them what you'll need to buy on a regular basis. If they want to keep you as a customer, they'll try to help. If they don't, take your business elsewhere.

In addition to shopping at grocery stores, check out health-food stores, co-ops, meat suppliers, butcher shops, Asian markets, local farmers and ranchers, farmers markets, and 4-H groups. Look in the phone book to find such businesses. Often, the same company that supplies your grocery store with meat will sell directly to you. Also check the Internet for what you need—you may be surprised by what you find! If you want to grind meat and/or bone yourself, you can check online for meat grinders or ask your butcher for recommendations.

The very best meat you can buy will be naturally raised, grass- or pasture-fed and finished, organic-meat animals. But if that's not available or not in your budget, just buy regular human-grade meat like you feed your human family. Personally, if I want ground meat, I often purchase one-pound tubes (called "chubs") of free-range ground turkey; I buy a case at a time because it's cheaper. If I can't afford the free-range stuff, I get the regular ground-turkey chubs. Occasionally, I purchase ground whole rabbit online. I also have a friend who shares her goat meat with me and another friend who has green-tripe parties! If I want whole birds or animals, I watch for sales on fryer chickens, Cornish game hens, and the like. When I cut up Cornish game hens into halves or quarters and feed them to the cats, they find it very exciting!

2. Organ meat. Check the same sources as you used for the preceding item. If the grocery store doesn't have them in the meat case, ask them to order what you need. Try to incorporate some heart in your cat's meal every day; a very small amount of liver is also good. As always, use the best quality you can find and afford.

Let's Go Shopping! 119

3. Bones. Of course, if you're using entire animals or whole bone-in pieces, ground or not, you won't need to purchase this ingredient separately. But if you need to buy separate bones, chicken or Cornish-game-hen necks are usually a good start. You can feed these whole with the rest of the meal or put them in already ground up. If you don't want to jump right into buying a grinder, necks are pretty easy to just smash with a hammer.

Sources for necks and other bones are basically the same as those suggested under muscle meat. Even if you don't see them at the meat counter (and you probably won't), your butcher or meat manager can order them (or you can buy directly from the supplier). For my own furry family, I purchase an entire case of organic chicken necks at a time. If they don't have any or if my wallet is thin, I get nonorganic ones by the case—but I must tell you that the organic ones sure look yummier.

I break the case up into smaller portions and freeze what I'm not going to use that week. As I put the necks away, I tear off and throw away the huge blob of fat that's usually attached to them since it would be too much for a cat. Even after I rip off the big piece of fat, there's still a little of it left on the neck, which is a more appropriate amount for feline tummies. If you're buying bonemeal powder instead of raw bones, it should be fit for human consumption and tested free of lead and other contaminants.

4. Essential fatty acids. These supplements are so popular now that you should have no trouble obtaining a good one. You'll find them at grocery and health-food stores, on the Internet, and lots of other places. The most important thing to look for is quality. You want one that hasn't been extracted by heat or chemical processes; and the label on the fish-body oil should state that it's been tested free of PCBs, heavy metals, and other toxins. Evening-primrose and borage oils should indicate that they're also free of chemicals, pesticides, and toxins. Many brands meet these standards, so don't worry that you won't be able to get one.

You'll also find products that contain both fish-body oil and evening-primrose or borage oil. These are okay as long as they meet your quality requirements. These substances are easily damaged by heat, light, and oxygen, so don't keep them in a hot car or leave the cap off the bottle. Store them in the refrigerator.

5. Raw, shelled sunflower seeds. Make sure these are fresh, and you definitely don't want to use roasted or toasted seeds since heat damages the nutrients and makes them rancid. If you don't find these in raw form at your regular grocery store, check health-food stores and the Internet.

There are a few different tools you can use to grind them into a powder: grinders specifically made for seeds, nuts, and herbs; the traditional mortar and pestle (that's too much work for me!); food processors; and coffee grinders. My food processor is too big to catch the little seeds, so I use the type of coffee grinder that has a push-down lid and a blade that reduces the seeds to a nice fine powder, and I have a separate grinder for coffee beans. I don't want any cross-contamination since coffee is bad for cats. Keeping two little bean/seed grinders eliminates the chance that even some of the coffee oils might mix with the seeds. Fortunately, these small machines are quite inexpensive. Store your seeds in the refrigerator.

6. Dulse or kelp powder. These are very popular food supplements, so you shouldn't have much trouble finding these either. Check health-food and supplement stores and the Internet. You want these ingredients in powdered form and preferably organically grown. It's important that the one you choose has been tested free of heavy metals and other toxins. If it doesn't say so on the label, contact the company to be certain. Use the same scrutiny of quality if you choose to use an algae, such as spirulina, instead of dulse or kelp.

7. Plain gelatin powder. You're looking for the unflavored, unsweetened type—no strawberry Jell-O for the cats! (Hmmm, I wonder if they'd like meat Jell-O?) You'll find gelatin powder in the bulk section, in packages, and through the Internet. Just make certain that it's good quality with nothing else added (no MSG, please). Contact the company if you're not sure it's MSG free.

8. Calcium ascorbate powder. This can be found in the same places as many of the other ingredients. Buy it in powdered form and look for the label to state that it's hypoallergenic; isn't genetically modified; and contains no fillers, excipients, binders, starch, wheat, soy, dairy, yeast, colorings, flavorings, or preservatives. You may want to buy a small bottle because you won't be using much.

Tell Kitty You're Going Hunting!

Those are all the ingredients you'll need to purchase. You'll probably find that the meats (muscle and organ) and bone (unless you're using meat that includes it) will need to be purchased more frequently than the supplements since the latter will be used in such small amounts. How much it costs to feed your cat will be, in large part, up to your shopping skills; and you'll get more adept as you become more experienced. Watch for sales and bargains to keep costs down to a minimum. And if the diet helps reduce the vet bills, that's an extra bonus. You might just have to treat yourself and your cat to something special to celebrate! How about a new toy—maybe you both need a new stick with feathers on the end? After working up a good appetite by playing, let's see how we can entice your cat to try its new menu in the following chapter.

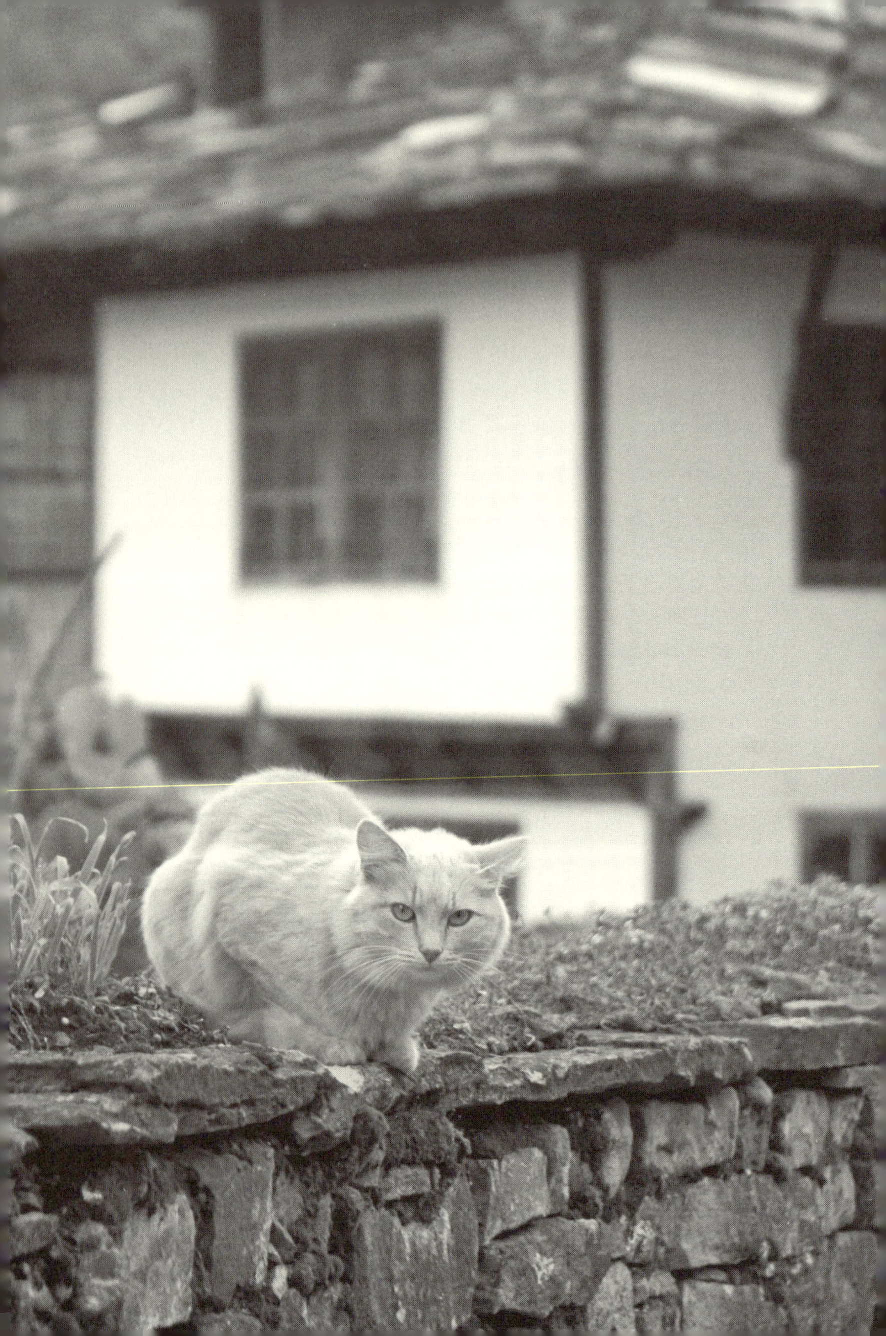

CHAPTER 11

Making the Switch

"After scolding one's cat, one looks into its face and is seized by the ugly suspicion that it understood every word. And has filed it for reference."
— Charlotte Gray

I've never known a cat that couldn't be switched to the raw diet, but I have known humans who gave up trying too soon. Some felines take to the new food right away, some cats require a little time to make the transition, and others may take quite a while before finally accepting it. As long as you're making forward progress—even if it feels like it's taking forever—you're headed in the right direction.

First things first: If you're "free-feeding" your cat by leaving kibble in its dish all day, stop right now! That's the very worst way to feed a cat. To begin with, you're exposing that kibble to additional oxidation and contamination. Second, you'll have an easier time controlling your cat's diet and health if you have specific mealtimes. Third, by leaving the food out all the time, you're overstimulating the digestive system. Fourth, I just have to repeat the fact that dry food is the very worst for your cat's health. In addition to the lousy ingredients, it's dehydrating and plays havoc with blood sugar.

If kibble is on the menu right now, put the bag somewhere new where the cat can't smell it. Don't get rid of it yet, as you may need it for the transition. After you've made a successful switch, however, throw that junk out!

If your cat doesn't accept raw food right away, don't give up. Don't take it personally and don't assume that your furry friend will always dislike it. Cats have an instinctual intelligence that makes them very suspicious of any new food. It's really very smart when you consider that in the wild, "Momcat" teaches her kittens what's safe to eat by introducing them to specific foods. They're programmed not to stray too far from the "approved"

Making the Switch

menu because eating something out of the norm could be fatal. So now it's up to you to convince and reassure them that what you're offering is indeed safe and good for them—and delicious once they give it a try!

I can't state emphatically enough that *your* attitude about the new food is of utmost importance in making a successful transition. Your cat can read you like a book, and if you act unsure about the food you're offering, they'll naturally be suspicious. You must serve meals with love and confidence.

You'll feed adult cats once or twice a day (kittens or pregnant cats more often). By giving one or two meals only at regular times, your cats will develop a hunger response. Leave the food down for about 30 minutes and then remove it; your cats will learn that they need to eat when you feed them. Also, don't let your cats skip more than two meals. If they haven't eaten anything for 24 hours, give them something you know they will eat. This is especially important for fat cats as they can run into trouble by starvation. But once you get them on the raw diet, their weight issue will most likely resolve itself beautifully.

One of the many benefits of this diet is increased muscle tone and better weight (whether they're too fat or too thin). They won't need to eat as much of the raw food because they'll get better nutrition, so don't be surprised if they need smaller meals than before. Also keep in mind that some cats really need their privacy at mealtime, while others enjoy a little competition. Do what works best for your feline friend.

There are a few different methods for switching to the raw diet and knowing your cat will help you find the best way. One of the biggest mistakes is that people are so excited to begin the diet that they aren't patient enough to move at the cat's pace. Chicken and turkey are good meats to begin with; stick with the one your cat accepts first. Begin to vary the type of meat only after your cat has been eating its new diet for a while. Don't use any whole bones while your cat is still eating kibble; the two are incompatible. Always serve food at room temperature or only slightly warm, never cold or hot. Even though you might have to take your time transitioning your cat to its new diet, don't stop halfway; keep moving forward to feeding the complete recipes.

Here are a few more suggestions for switching your cat to its new diet. Try one at a time and maintain patience and a good attitude:

Making the Switch

1. Test the water by jumping right in and offering the new diet. If your cat eats it, congratulations—you're done!

2. Begin offering teeny tiny pieces of raw meat, either off your finger, mixed with the cat's old food, or next to it in the dish.

3. In a separate bowl, pour a little boiling water over a tiny piece of meat. This will slightly parboil it and release more aroma. (One of the reasons cats get hooked on certain foods is by smell association.) After it's cooled, offer it as recommended in Tip 2.

4. Coat a tiny piece of raw meat with one of the bribe foods mentioned following this list or with their old food.

5. Mix a really tiny piece of raw meat into your cat's regular food. If this is accepted, gradually increase the size of the new ingredient while decreasing the old diet.

6. Make a single serving size of either Recipe #3 or Recipe #4 (which you'll find later in the book) and use the above techniques to gradually introduce it into your cat's current diet. Very lightly cook it if you have to, and then cook it less and less until it's raw. Increase the amount of this new food only as much as your cat is comfortable with.

7. Switch your cat to a better-quality commercial canned food, then transition to the raw diet.

Use bribe foods to help with any of the above suggestions. These may include anything your cat really likes, such as: meat baby food (no onion/garlic—see Chapter 13), freeze-dried liver treats, ground cooked or raw meat made mushy with warm water, and anything else your cat loves that won't hurt it during the transition. As your cat makes the switch, very slowly decrease the bribe foods.

If you're making large batches of the C.A.T. diet and freezing extra meal-sized portions, defrost these as you would for yourself: Place the container in the refrigerator overnight, soak it in cold water for a few hours, or submerge it in warm water to speed the process. If the food is still chilled, add a little hot water to bring it to room temperature.

Also feel free to use different meats than called for in the recipes I'll provide. If the recipe specifies chicken but you got a good deal on turkey or whatever, use it!

Dishes

Don't use plastic dishes for food or water. They may outgas (give off) chemicals or contribute scraped-off bits of plastic to your cat's diet, and they don't clean up as well as other materials. Aluminum is out, too. Better choices include glass or ceramic dishes—just make sure they're lead free. If a ceramic dish cracks, lead may be underneath the glaze, so it should be replaced. Know your cat: Some like bowls, and many others prefer plates. Giving each cat its own dish enables you to keep track of how much each feline is eating.

Detox

It may never happen to your cat, but it should be mentioned that some animals do a little "housecleaning" when they begin to eat healthy food. For example, if they've got a lot of mucus in their intestines, you may see it in their stools (along with any resident worms being given the boot) as their body becomes healthier. If they're on medication, you'll want to recheck whether the amount being given is still accurate after they've been on their new diet for a while. As their body increases in health, they may need the dosage lowered. A digestive enzyme and/or probiotic for cats may help if they develop an upset tummy. What you'll probably notice most about your feline friends after they've been eating well for a bit is brighter eyes and more feel-good energy.

Oh, Poop!

Once your cat is eating its new raw-food diet, you'll probably find small, firm stools in its litter box. Hooray, less to clean up! And it also means that more food is being utilized, so less waste is being produced. Here's the scoop on poop: Too much organ meat or vitamin C may loosen stools, while too much bone will harden them. This knowledge will help you get the diet just right for your individual cat should its poop go one way or the other.

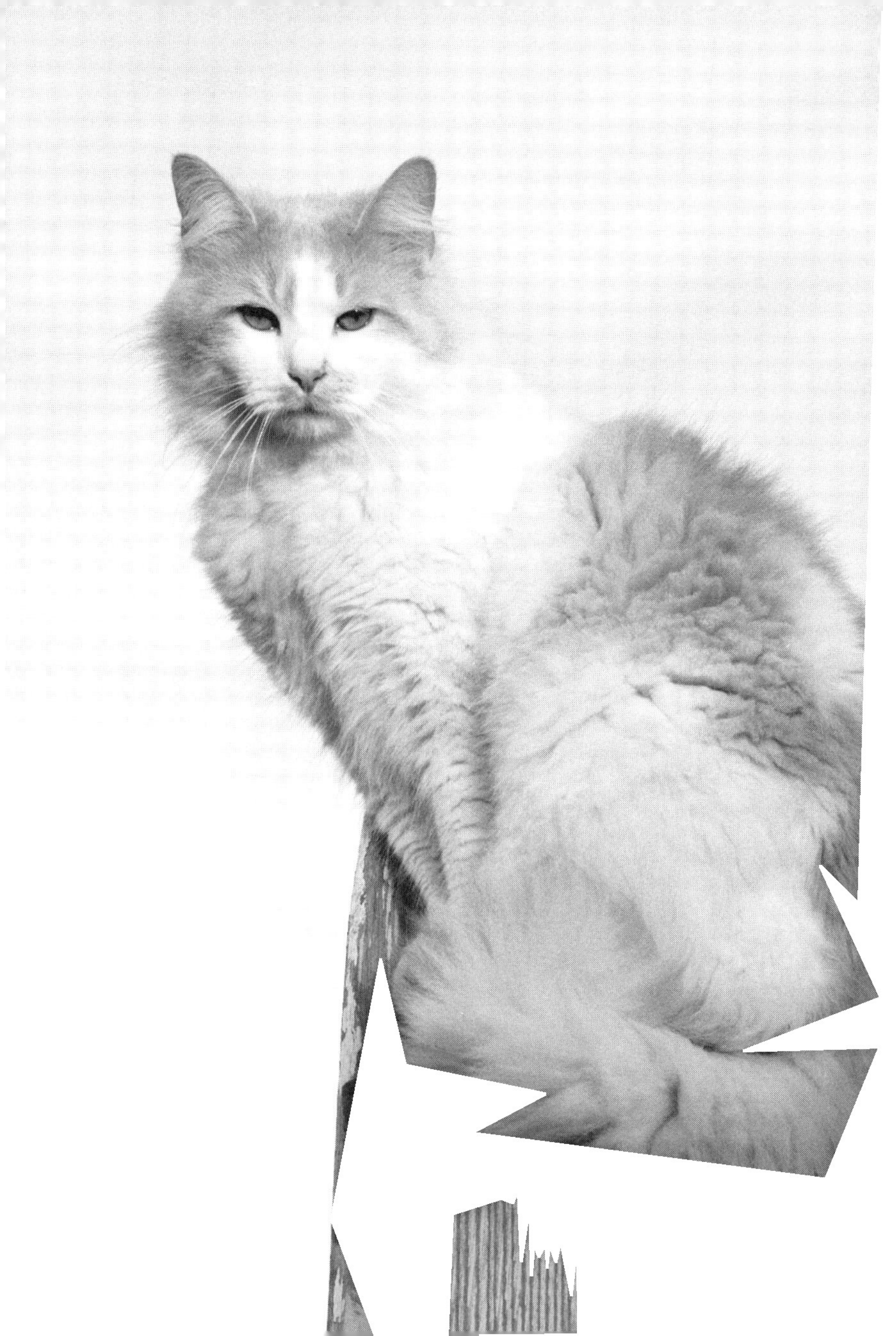

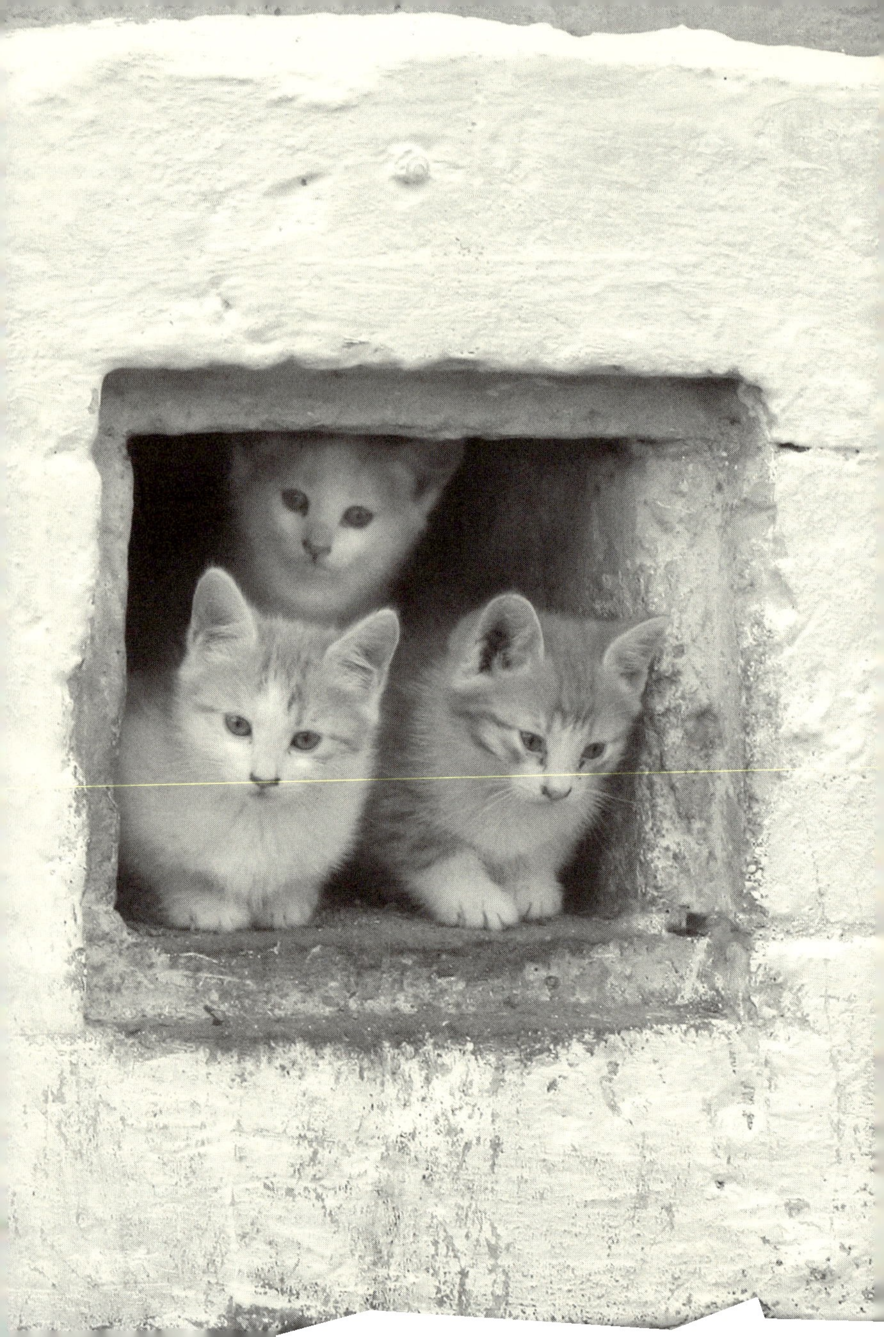

CHAPTER 12

Special Needs and Life Stages

"The smallest feline is a masterpiece."
— Leonardo da Vinci

A species-appropriate diet of raw food offers cats of any age a great foundation for health. The notion of special products being needed based on age, breed, gender, or whether your cat lives indoors is a marketing gimmick used by pet-food companies. Sure, a very active young cat may need to consume more food than a couch potato, but it certainly doesn't require different formulations. In the wild, there are no special "kitten mice" or "active-formula birds." Nope, the feline predator in nature eats what it catches at any age. The only variations we need to make to the homemade diet will be to change the size of each meal or the frequency of feeding.

Moms and Kittens

Pregnant cats will need to eat smaller, more frequent meals since her young share her nourishment and take up more space in her body. Lactating cats will also need more in order to supply ample milk. I prefer to let kittens nurse for as long as Mom allows; and as long as she's receiving enough food, she should be able to keep up her condition as well as provide for her babies. On the C.A.T. diet, I've found that mama cats can maintain their condition beautifully while feeding many youngsters. As the kittens are weaned, her meals will gradually be reduced back to one or two a day. Kittens burn up a lot of calories and will need to eat small frequent meals, perhaps four to six per day. By the time they're six months old, they may be down to three meals per day, and then drop back to two when they're a year old.

Seniors

Older cats don't require specialized food either. They need a good nutrient-dense diet such as the one recommended in this book. You may notice that they eat less at each meal, which is fine as long as they maintain good weight and condition. That shouldn't be a problem since cats of all ages thrive on good nutrition. I hear over and over that older cats look and act very young for their age when they eat a well-made raw diet.

Disease

This isn't a medical text, and I'll leave the diagnosis and treatment of disease up to you and your cat's health practitioner. But as far as diet considerations for cats with illnesses, I will say that good nutrition is so very important for prevention and supporting your cat's health. The best you can do nutritionally for any disease is to offer a species-appropriate diet—that means one without ingredients that felines shouldn't have, such as grains.

Remember, once eaten, grains break down into sugar within your cat's body, which contributes to numerous health problems, including diabetes, cancer, and many others. In fact, cancer cells thrive on sugar. Speaking of that illness, one of many important nutrients for your cat that a raw diet offers is conjugated linoleic acid (CLA). Studies show that it may help protect against cancer, increase bone mass, and have a positive effect on diabetes. This nutrient is found in raw meat.

Treats

Any chapter on special needs would be remiss if it didn't mention treats! Although not absolutely necessary, they're fun to give our cats and help us create a special bond with them. These days, cat treats abound in pet-food stores, and some of these are fine to give occasionally. The favorites around here are definitely the freeze-dried liver and other meat treats. Just check the label to be certain that no other ingredients—including preservatives—have been added. The same goes for any special snack you find at the store; check the ingredients carefully, and exclude any with grains

Special Needs and Life Stages

and other carbohydrates or any substance your cat shouldn't eat.

Pots of wheatgrass are very popular with many cats. You can grow your own or purchase a container of it at your local health-food store. Mist it with water every so often and throw it out if you notice any mold. Lots of kitties love to nibble on the grass, and it's good for them, too. Well-known nutritional pioneer Ann Wigmore of the Hippocrates Institute was a big proponent of wheatgrass and fed it regularly to the cats at the institute with very good results. I suggest weighting the pot down so that it stays where you want it. I had one cat who thought it was very amusing to grab the grass and drag the entire pot around the house, leaving a trail of dirt as she went! After that, we learned to anchor it.

Another source for treats is my book *The Natural Nutrition No-Cook Book: Delicious Food for You . . . and Your Pets!* You'll find easy recipes for wonderful healthy treats for the whole family—human and feline!

One more suggestion is to never forget the "treat" of play and interaction! Play with and talk to your cat regularly. There are all sorts of great toys out there, but do make sure that any items you choose are big enough not to be swallowed.

The favorite at our house is a stick with feathers on the end—we have some champion leapers! Of course, just as popular is a paper bag with one corner torn out, and it's definitely better priced!

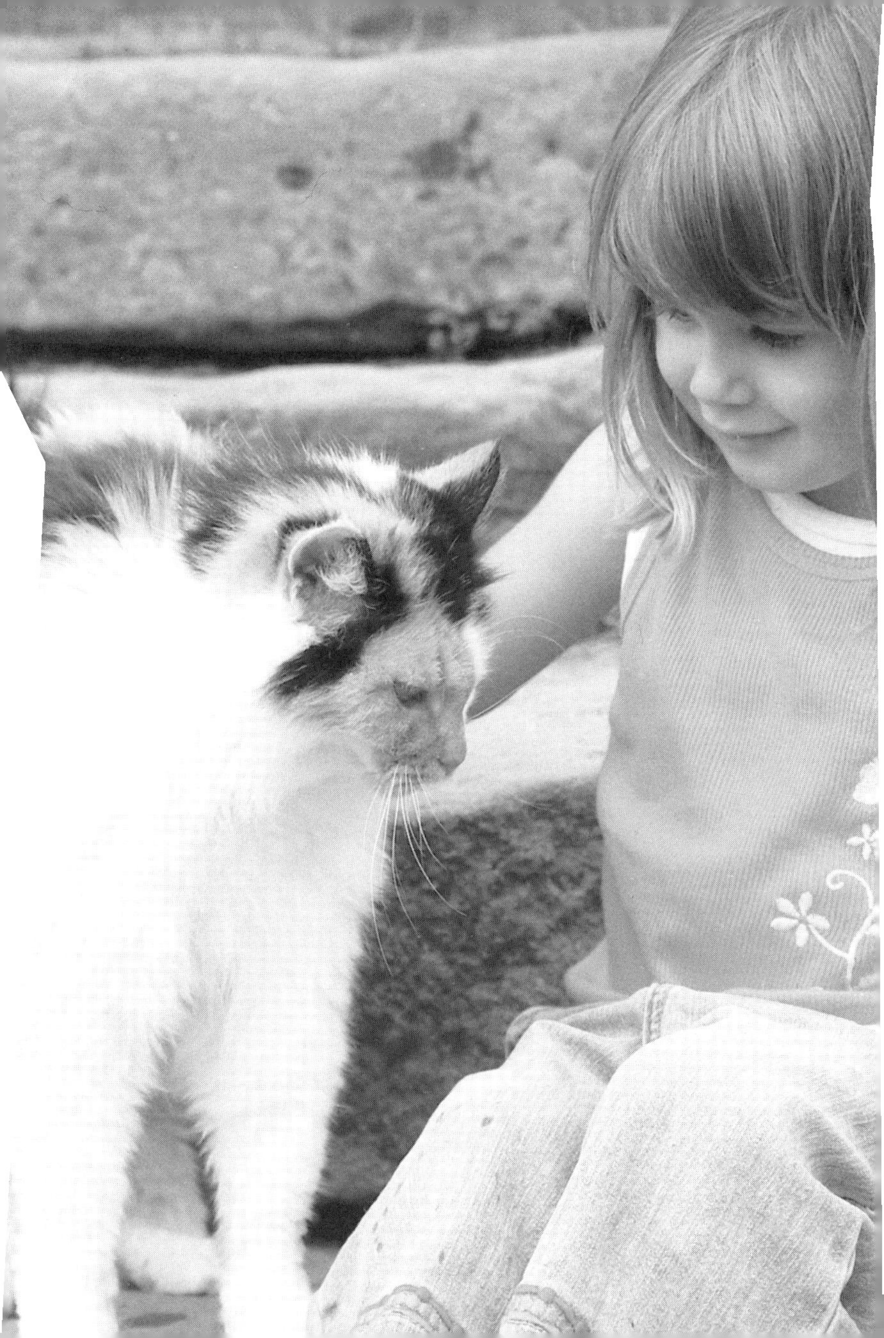

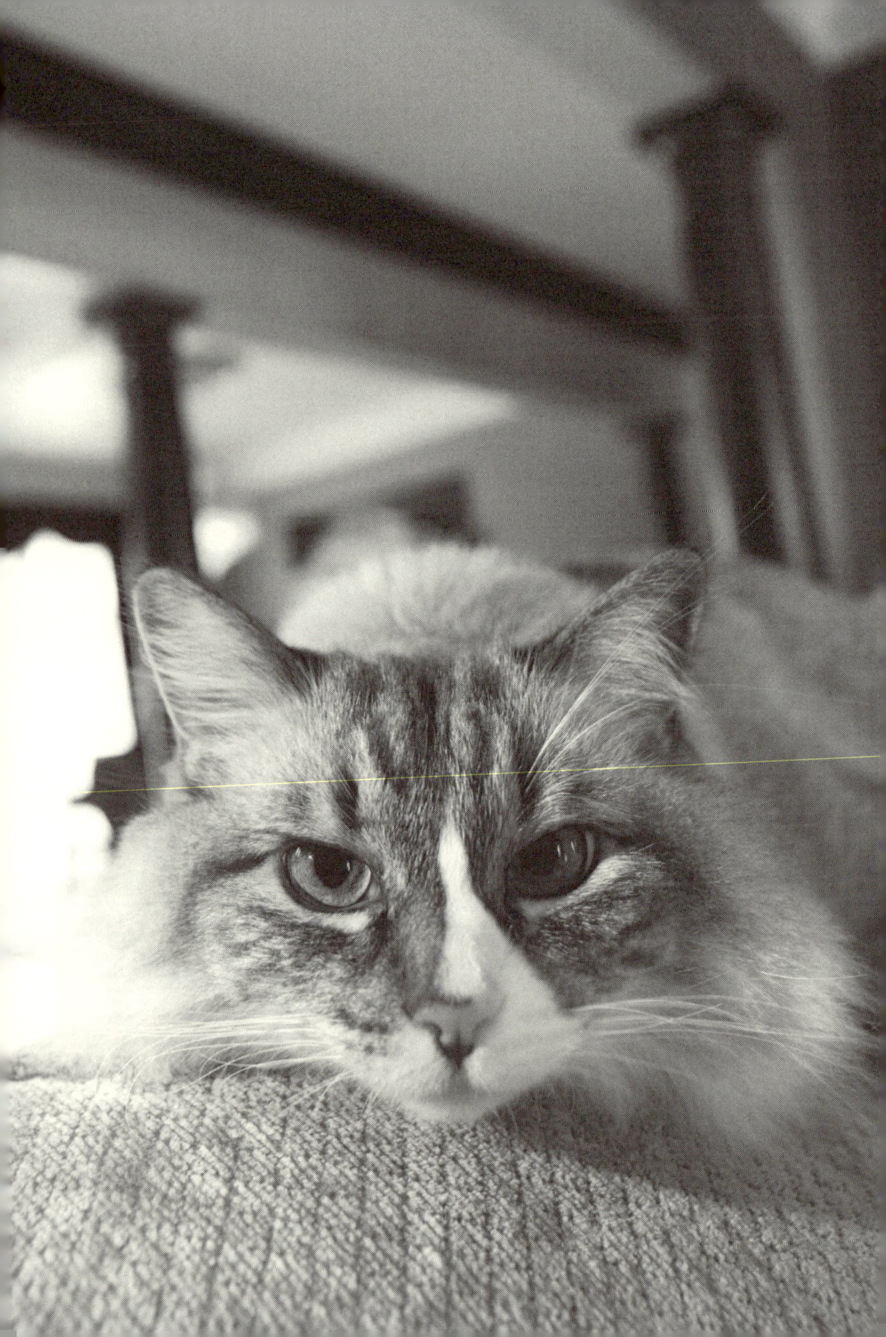

CHAPTER 13

Use Caution with Cats

"There are two means of refuge from the miseries of life: music and cats."
— Albert Schweitzer

This is by no means a list of everything on the planet that's bad for cats, but it's a few of the things that should be avoided by themselves or as an ingredient in something else:

— **Alpha lipoic acid.** Also referred to as *lipoic acid*, this is an antioxidant that increases production of glutathione and can cause gastrointestinal distress and low blood sugar in cats.

— **Chocolate.** This contains the alkaloid theobromine, which is toxic to cats. It also contains caffeine and may have sugar.

— **Dairy.** This includes milk, cream, butter, cheese, cottage cheese, yogurt, whey, sour cream, kefir, casein, and ice cream. Milk is a hormonal growth fluid produced by a mother for her young of the same species. Cats don't "milk" cows (or mice) and, after weaning, have no need for dairy products. A weaned cat isn't equipped with the enzymes needed to digest the protein and sugar in dairy products. Plus, studies with felines show that casein (a protein in milk) interferes with the absorption of other nutrients.

— **Drugs.** No, not all drugs, of course, but many that are safe (relatively speaking) for other animals are very harmful to cats. Examples include aspirin, acetaminophen, antihistamines, decongestants, ibuprofen, NSAIDs, salicylates, and sodium phosphate enemas. Always be certain that any drug you're considering is specifically safe for cats, and always check the drug insert, with your vet, or a reputable Website for possible side effects and contraindications.

— **Dry cat food.** As mentioned elsewhere in this book, commercial dry food is totally unsuitable for felines. It's dehydrating and high in carbohydrates, and both these qualities spell disaster. It definitely does not clean teeth and may, in fact, contribute to tartar. Just say no.

— **Essential oils.** Cats are very sensitive to the potent essential oils that may be used around other animals, including humans. If you wish to use aromatherapy for your cats, look into the more dilute hydrosols. Use caution with cleaning products that contain essential oils, and make certain your cat doesn't get into potpourri.

— **Grains.** Cats have absolutely no nutritional requirement for any types of grains. They aren't a natural food for felines and contribute to many health problems. They're also a source of sugar, which is another substance that should always be avoided.

— **Grapes and raisins.** These are tricky because no one is certain yet why there have been recent reports of toxicity due to grape and raisin ingestion. Until we know more, they're best avoided.

— **Houseplants.** There are too many plants that are toxic to cats to name here. Some aren't poisonous, but personally, I presume one *is* until I find out otherwise. Let your cat know that the only plant it may call its own is a nice pot of wheatgrass or "cat grass."

— **Herbs.** Let me be very clear that not all herbs are bad for cats, but because quite a few aren't recommended for them, I want to make sure that you check an herbal reference book for cats to be certain the ones you're interested in are safe for felines. There are many wonderful herbs that can be very useful in cat health, but be sure they're specifically approved for cats.

— **Microwave oven.** I know many of you are extremely attached to your microwave ovens, but please don't use them to defrost or warm your cat's food. I hate to break the news, but there's a huge amount of research proving that they change foods to the detriment of health. Sorry, but it's true. Did you know that it's reported that hospitals don't microwave blood or baby formula because it can have fatal results? These appliances change the molecular structure of food and significant changes in the blood are seen after microwaved food is ingested. Microwave ovens have actually been banned in some other countries due to their danger to health. This controversial subject could fill an entire book, so for more information check out the Price-Pottenger Nutrition Foundation; they're one good source available for up-to-date microwave-oven information.

— **Onions and garlic.** Ingestion of these foods are related to destruction of red blood cells, and they may also irritate the gastrointestinal system. There's still debate about the harmful effects of garlic because many people—including holistic vets—have used it in cats without problems, but I want to inform you of the potential risk. Our cats could probably ward off a vampire without the aid of garlic, anyway!

— **Raw salmon.** Salmon poisoning is an infectious disease caused by a rickettsia that uses a parasitic fluke on the fish as a host. It can cause serious illness and death.

— **Soy.** This is found in various forms in many products. It contains compounds that may negatively affect cats by interfering with nutrient absorption, normal growth, thyroid function, and hormonal development.

— **Sugar.** As discussed earlier, cancer cells thrive on this, as do many other disease processes. Sugar comes in many forms, including beet, raw, brown, cane, fructose, corn sweetener, corn syrup, date, dextrin, dextrose, glucose, lactose, maltose, manitol, polydextrose, sorbitol, sorghum, sucanat, sucrose, turbinado, barley malt, molasses, honey, and maple syrup. Xylitol, a sweetener made from carbohydrates, should also be avoided.

— **Yeast.** This is a fungus that many cats can't tolerate; it may cause allergic reactions, bloating, and digestive and urinary problems. Different forms include brewer's, nutritional, baker's, torula, and primary yeasts.

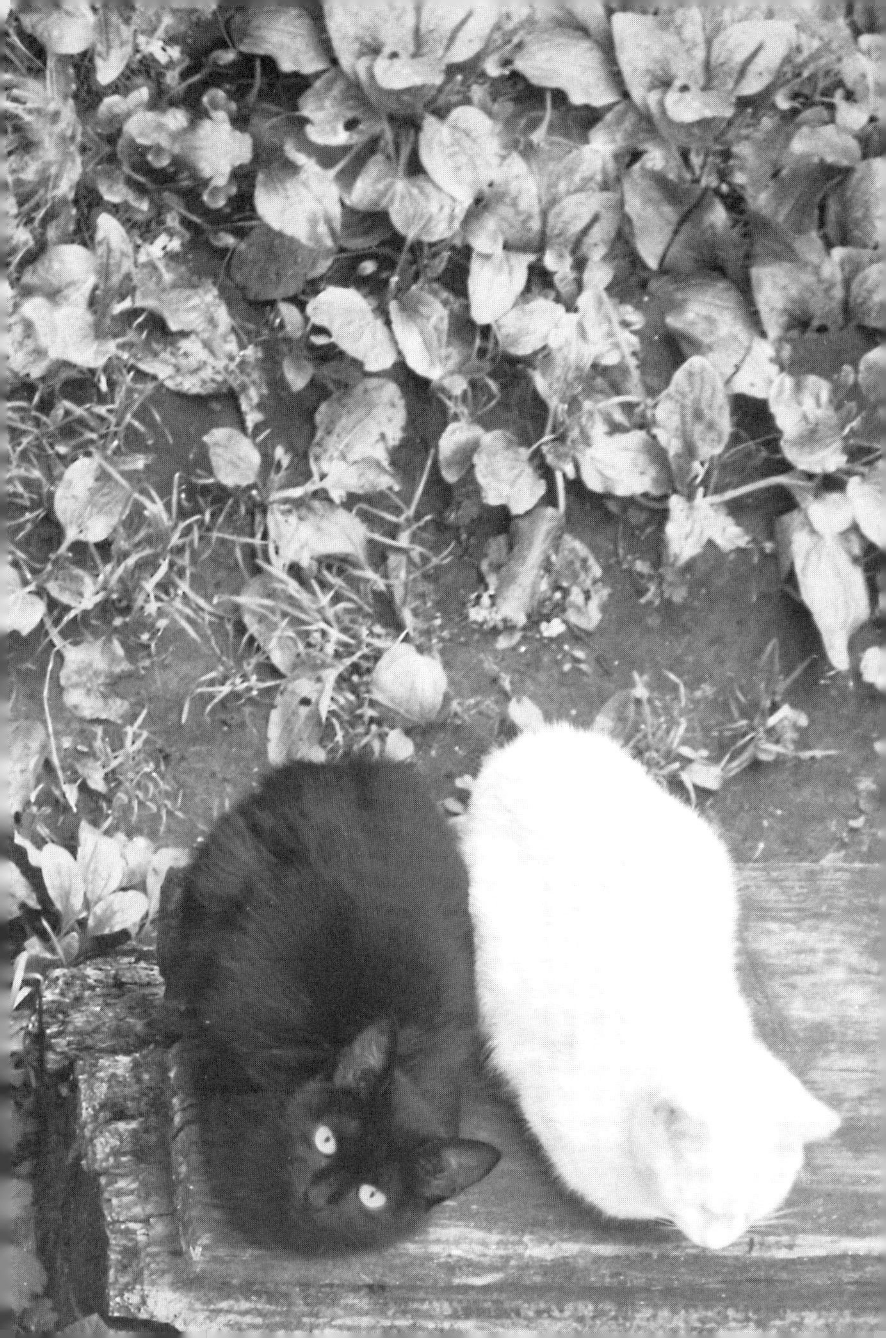

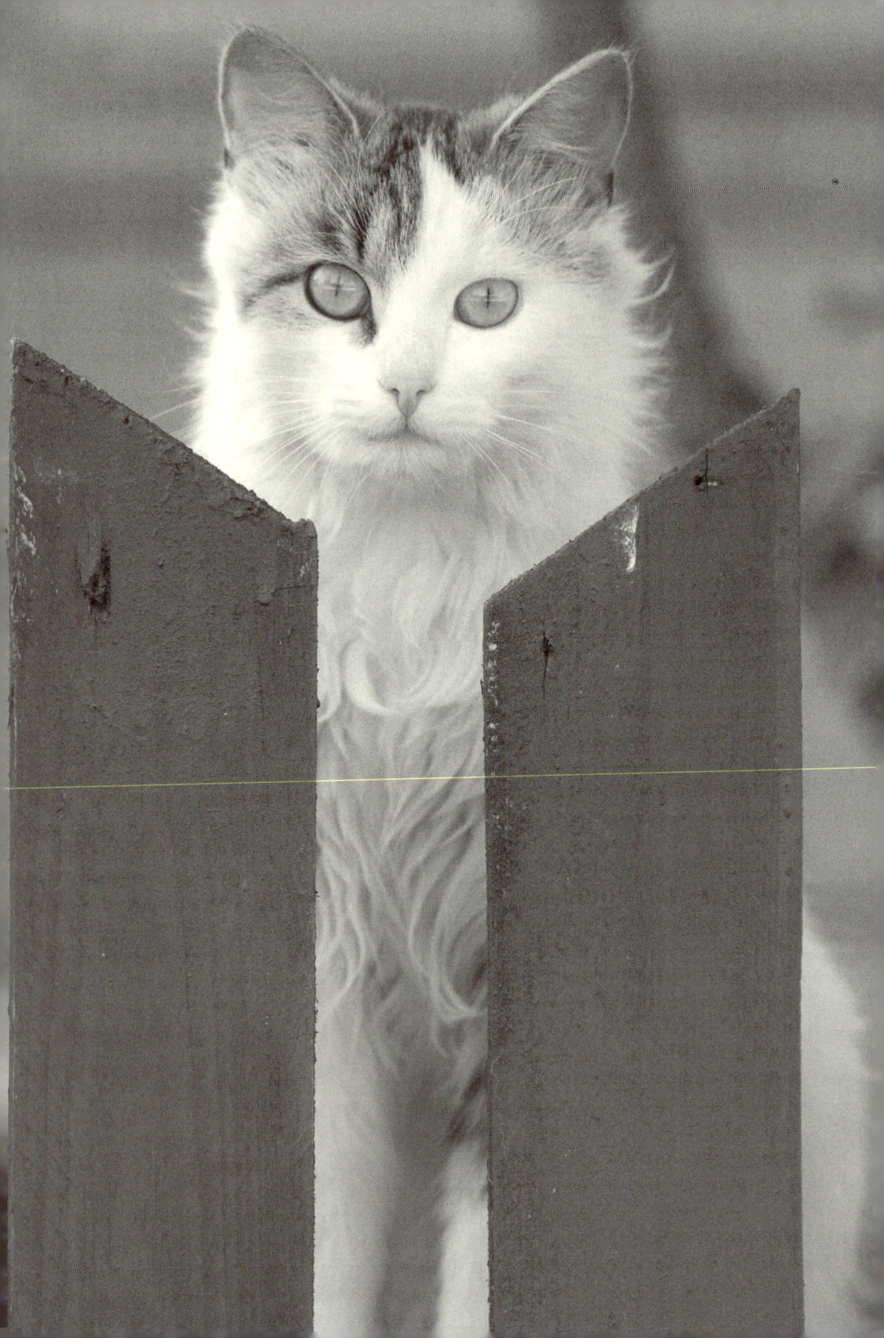

CHAPTER 14

C.A.T. Diet Recipes

Recipe #1

- 1 raw Cornish game hen
- 1 raw heart
- 1 small piece of raw liver (preferably from the hen; if not, use about 1 heaping Tbsp.)
- 1 raw egg
- 1 tsp. fish-body oil (approximately 1,000 mg) or replace ¼ tsp. of the fish oil with evening-primrose oil or borage oil for a combination of oils
- 2 tsp. Super Supp (recipe at the end of this chapter)

Cut or chop the hen into quarters.

— **Option 1.** Quarter the heart and liver. In a bowl, blend egg, oil(s), and Super Supp. Place ¼ hen, ¼ heart, and ¼ liver in cat's dish with ¼ of the egg/oil/Supp mixture.

— **Option 2.** Chop heart and liver into very small pieces and blend with the egg/oil/Supp mixture. Serve ¼ of mixture alongside ¼ hen.

— **Option 3.** Coat ¼ hen in ¼ of the egg/oil blend and then coat with ½ tsp. Super Supp.

— **Option 4.** Mix ¼ of the egg/oil blend with ½ tsp. of Super Supp and serve alongside ¼ hen.

Serve all of these options at room temperature. Bye-bye, Birdie!

Serving options per meal based on two meals per day for the average adult cat. This recipe should provide four meals—two days' worth of food—but that totally depends on how much your cat eats. Increase or decrease amounts evenly as necessary for your cat or if you wish to prepare a bulk batch.

If ¼ hen is too much food for one meal, chop the hen into smaller pieces. If needed, you may rub some freeze-dried liver or other bribe food on the hen to get your cat started. Once it takes that first bite, the taste of the food usually leads to an empty dish.

If you don't care to have the bones whole, take a hammer and smash the heck out of them. If you feed your cat this dish every day, you may want to omit the egg every so often.

Recipe #2

- 1 pound ground chicken or whole boneless chicken parts (about 2 cups)
- 8 or 9 chicken necks with the blob of fatty skin pulled off (if they came with it)
- 2 chicken hearts
- 2 oz. chicken liver (about ¼ cup)
- 2 tsp. (approximately 2,000 mg) fish-body oil or replace ¼ tsp. of the fish oil with evening-primrose oil or borage oil for a combination of oils
- 4 tsp. Super Supp (recipe at the end of this chapter)

Chop or puree the hearts and liver. If using whole boneless chicken, cut into nickel-size pieces.

— **Option 1.** Combine all ingredients except necks in large bowl and blend thoroughly. At mealtime, spoon approximately ¼ cup into cat's dish. If it's too stiff for your cat's taste (many prefer their food a little mushy) add a little warm water. If it's coming straight out of the fridge, add hot water and blend. Serve at room temperature. After your cat has finished eating the meat mix, give it one chicken neck for dessert.

— **Option 2.** Grind all the necks and blend with other ingredients. Serve as described in Option 1.

— **Option 3.** Make Option 1, then grind one chicken neck and add to the individual meal. Serve as described in Option 1 (minus "dessert").

— **Option 4.** Make Option 1 and serve as described. Smash one chicken neck (still leaving it whole) and give for dessert after the individual meal.

This recipe makes approximately eight meals of ¼ cup each and should provide food for the average adult cat for four or five days. Your mileage may vary, depending on how much your cat eats per meal. You may rub the necks with freeze-dried liver or some other bribe food to introduce them to your cat if it doesn't recognize them as food at first. If you feed this meal often, occasionally add an egg.

Recipe #3

- 10 lbs. (approximately) of bone-in whole meat such as chicken, turkey, rabbit, etc. organ meat that came with the whole meat (approximately 2½ cups)
- 2 eggs with shells
- 3 Tbsp. fish-body oil (approximately 9,000 mg) or
- 2 Tbsp. fish and 1 Tbsp. evening-primrose oil or borage oil
- ¾ cup plus 1 Tbsp. Super Supp (recipe at the end of this chapter)

Grind the meat and eggs, then simply combine with the other ingredients in a very large bowl. Divide into meal-size containers. Store what you'll use in the next couple of days in the refrigerator and freeze the rest. When you serve it, add a little warm or hot water to bring it to room temperature and adjust the consistency to your cat's liking.

Obviously this is a big batch recipe. You'll need to either grind the whole bone-in meat yourself or have your butcher do it for you. Ground, whole bone-in animals may also be purchased through various sources. If the muscle meat didn't come with organ meat, just use some from the same type of animal, or if that's not possible, any organ meat available.

If your cat eats ¼ cup of food twice daily, this recipe makes enough to last the average adult cat about 20 days or almost three weeks, depending how much your cat eats. The organ-meat mixture should include heart.

Recipe #4

1 lb. ground meat (2 cups)
2 hearts (about ¼ cup)
2 oz. liver (about ¼ cup)
1 egg with shell (occasionally)

C.A.T. Diet Recipes

- 2 tsp. (approximately 2,000 mg) fish-body oil or replace ¼ tsp. of the fish oil with evening-primrose oil or borage oil for a combination of oils
- 4 tsp. Super Supp (recipe at the end of this chapter)
- 1 Tbsp. bonemeal

Simply put all ingredients into a large food processor and blend thoroughly, or just put them in a big bowl and use your hands to mix well. It will be like making a giant meatloaf. If you don't like touching raw meat, you can wear dish gloves. Serve at room temperature, adding warm or hot water if your cat prefers a softer texture.

This recipe makes approximately eight meals of ¼ cup each and should provide food for the average adult cat for four or five days. You may increase all amounts equally to make a big batch; freeze what won't be used in about three days.

Vary the recipe by adding or subtracting the egg and using different meats. When making the food without the eggshell, add another teaspoon of bonemeal.

"Super Supp" Recipe

½ cup plain, unflavored gelatin powder
½ cup kelp or dulse powder
½ cup ground, raw, shelled sunflower seeds
2 tsp. calcium-ascorbate powder
1 heaping Tbsp. ground freeze-dried liver or heart (optional, but very tasty!)

Grind sunflower seeds into a powder. It will take slightly less than ½ cup of whole sunflower seeds to make ½ cup of powder. Also grind a couple of freeze-dried liver or heart pieces in the same grinder. (Of course, you'll wipe the grinder clean when you're finished.)

Combine all ingredients in a bowl and blend thoroughly, or put in a glass jar with a tight-fitting lid (mason jars work well) and shake to blend. Store in an airtight, moisture-proof glass container in the refrigerator and use within six months.

Recipe can be adjusted to your needs by increasing or decreasing all ingredients proportionately. I can't stress enough how important it is that the components of this recipe be of the very highest quality.

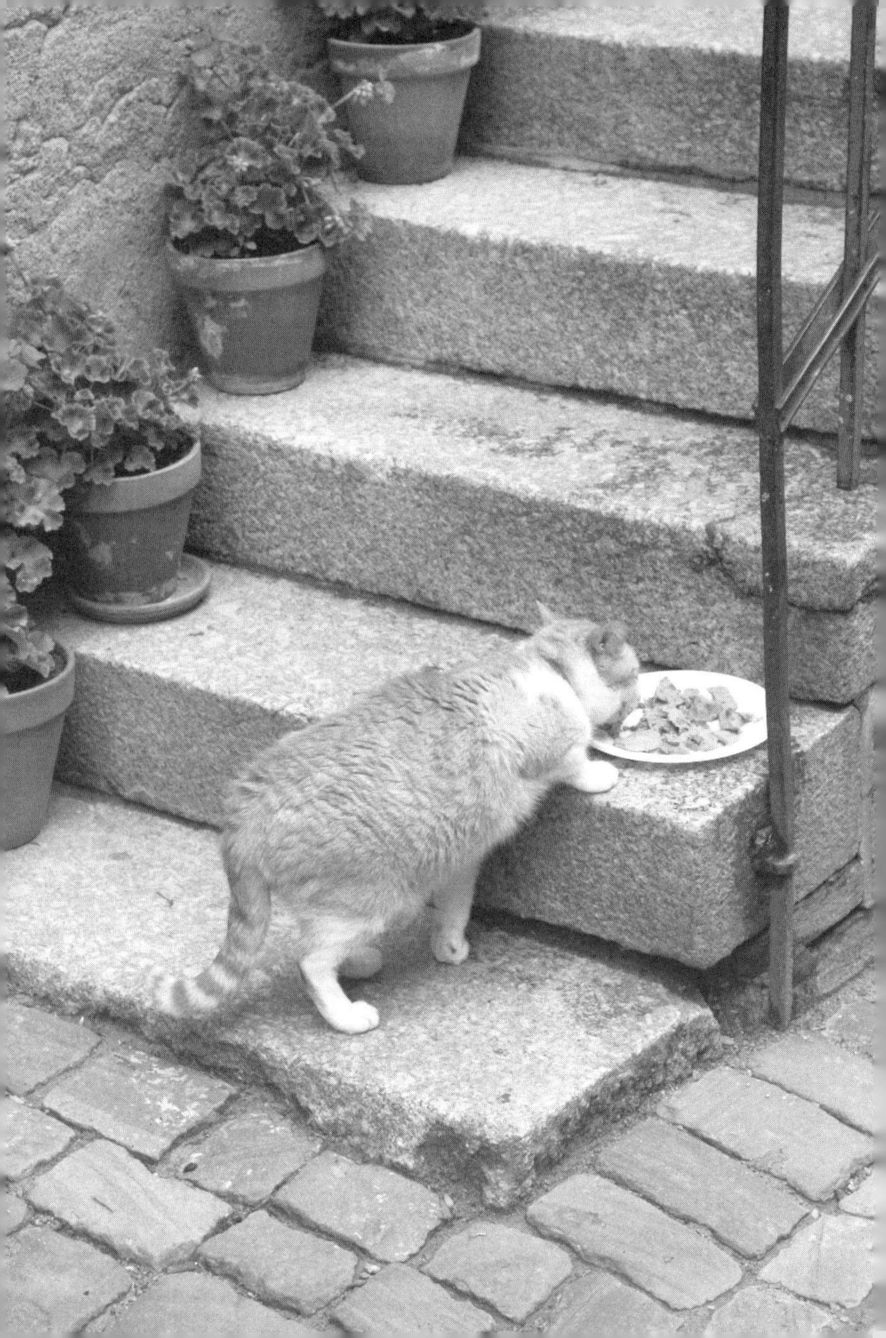

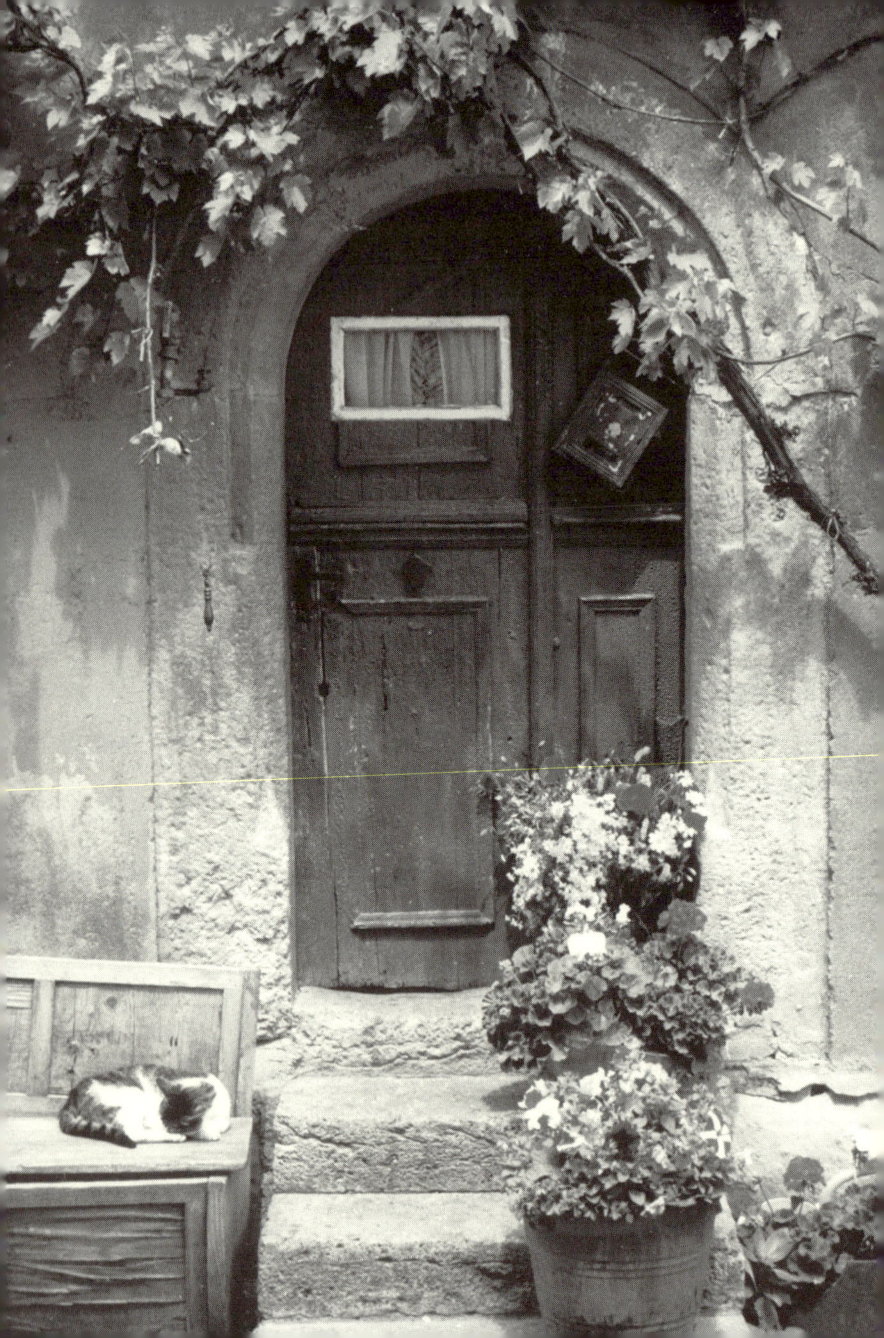

CHAPTER 15

Holistic Health Care

"I love cats because I enjoy my home; and little by little, they become its visible soul."
— Jean Cocteau

The root of the word *holistic* comes from the Greek word *holos* meaning *all, entire, total*. The general principle is that all properties of a system can't be determined or explained by the sum of its component parts alone. Instead, the system as a whole determines how the parts behave. Aristotle summarized holism succinctly by explaining: "The whole is more than the sum of its parts." Examples of this philosophy are found throughout history in diverse contexts, including biology.

It's really amusing that some folks consider *holistic* to be a "New Age" term, when in fact it's quite "old age"! In terms of health care for our cats, it refers to considering the well-being of the complete animal, not simply its individual parts. For example, a cat's respiratory system isn't more important than its gastrointestinal or cardiovascular system, and treating them as separate entities misses the fact that they're connected.

Every system and part of your cat works with the others to form good or bad health. If one of them is affected by disease, it will, in turn, affect the entire cat. To put it more simply, to look at your cat's health holistically means to consider the whole enchilada, the complete being. Feeding a species-appropriate diet is one way of treating your cat holistically because you know that the good food you're putting in its tummy will have a positive effect on the rest of its body.

Thinking of your cat's health in this manner considers all things that affect your furry friend. For example, exercise and sunshine are important to its overall well-being, so please make sure that it gets plenty of both. Playing with your cat is a great way to make sure it receives enough exercise, plus it's a fun way to bond. As for sunshine, living outdoors can be very dangerous for felines, so you'll need to be creative with your indoor kitty. Building an indoor/outdoor enclosure isn't difficult and will fulfill the need for sunlight, fresh air, stimulation, and perhaps even batting around a few bugs that wander in. A simply built coop can be attached to your house at a window, thereby allowing you to open it when you're home to supervise and closing it otherwise. When open, cats can go in and out as they please.

Another important consideration for your cat's holistic health are the chemicals it may come in contact with inside your home. Cigarette smoke, household cleaners, detergents, pesticides, insecticides (including flea products), and carpet and paint fumes are just a few of the dangerous toxins that can have a negative impact on your cat's health. Over-vaccination is also a major health concern, so make certain your vet is up-to-date on the latest research and always ask to read the paper insert that comes with the vaccines. You have the right to this information, and you should be concerned if a vet doesn't understand or comply with your request.

The material used in your cat's litter box should also be carefully considered. Even though the information is anecdotal, I'll tell you that when I worked in a busy veterinary clinic, I assisted in quite a few surgeries to remove impactions of clumping cat litter from feline intestines. There are many types of litter available, so please investigate thoroughly before you decide which is best for your cat. Be sure to keep the litter box clean and in a private yet accessible place. Also keep in mind that some cats prefer a box with a low rim and some don't.

Remember, anything that gets on the outside of a cat usually winds up on the inside, too. Also, holistic health care takes mental well-being into account, so please spend quality time with your cats. Bond, play, groom, and talk to your kitties. You never know what they might say back to you!

Veterinarians

Since we're discussing feline health care, let's talk just a bit about veterinarians. When you consider the benefits of a holistic perspective, you may understand why many people choose to take their cats to holistic-minded vets. Ideally, these medical professionals look at our cats' health in a comprehensive manner (considering the health of the entire animal, not just its "parts") and treat them with healing modalities that increase their overall well-being. Actually, a vet doesn't have to advertise as being holistic to think that way.

There are many reasons to choose a particular veterinarian. You may want to go to a cat-only clinic or at least to someone who's up-to-date on feline-health issues. When I choose a vet, I ideally want to find one who's either a proponent of raw diets or at least respects me as a responsible guardian who is capable of making intelligent decisions. I have little patience for vets totally against raw diets, telling me they're dangerous or too difficult to execute. What if a physician told you that you weren't capable of feeding your own children? You'd probably find another doctor.

As for difficulty, that's really their own perception, not what I find to be the reality of creating easy-to-make meals for my cats. When vets say these things, I just have to wonder how they think cats survived before the recent invention of commercial pet foods. Have they considered how their grandparents or great-grandparents managed to keep cats alive? Additionally, if they're adamant in their opinion that raw diets are unsafe, they might use that as an excuse for any health issue my cat may have—whether it's really diet-related or not.

Here's a good example of the blind prejudice that some veterinarians have against raw-food diets:

I have a friend who took her elderly cat for a simple checkup. The vet raved about how he'd never seen a cat of that age (I believe the animal was in her 20s) that was so vibrant and healthy. He actually told my friend that the cat's blood work should be framed and hung on her wall because it was absolutely perfect—something he'd never seen at that age. All was happy and friendly until my friend happened to mention that her cat had eaten a raw diet for the majority of its life. The celebration came to a screeching halt as the vet told her that she must put the cat on a commercial food immediately because a raw diet would kill it. Hello, Einstein?

As for commercial pet food being safer than a well-prepared homemade diet, I might point out that there have been at *least* 16 recalls, involving hundreds of products, within the past 12 years—and those are just the ones that got press. Those foods hurt and killed many beloved family members, as did the ones that were deficient in taurine for many years. How many cats suffer from product-related illness that's never implicated by a mass recall or the discovery of nutritional inadequacy?

At this time, I have papers that list 70 reports and studies citing harm and death to pets caused by commercial processed pet-food products. You'll find them in veterinary and medical journals from around the world. Of course, nothing in life is without risk, and we must make decisions that we can live with. Could a cat eating a raw-food diet get sick? Yes. Could a cat eating a processed product get sick? Yes. But I choose the former because over the last two decades my cats have been healthier than they ever were on processed products. Plus, I feel better, too, because I have more control over their diet—and I'm not alone. So many people all over the world have enjoyed the same results.

When it comes down to it, every vet is as human as we all are, so look for one you get along with on a personal and professional level. See that their clinic is well organized and has good, up-to-date equipment. Not every holistic veterinarian is the cat's meow, and not every conventional practitioner is bad. They're just people, each entitled to their own opinion and bedside manner. Find an intelligent person you can relate to—who treats you with respect and your cat with kindness and skilled veterinary care.

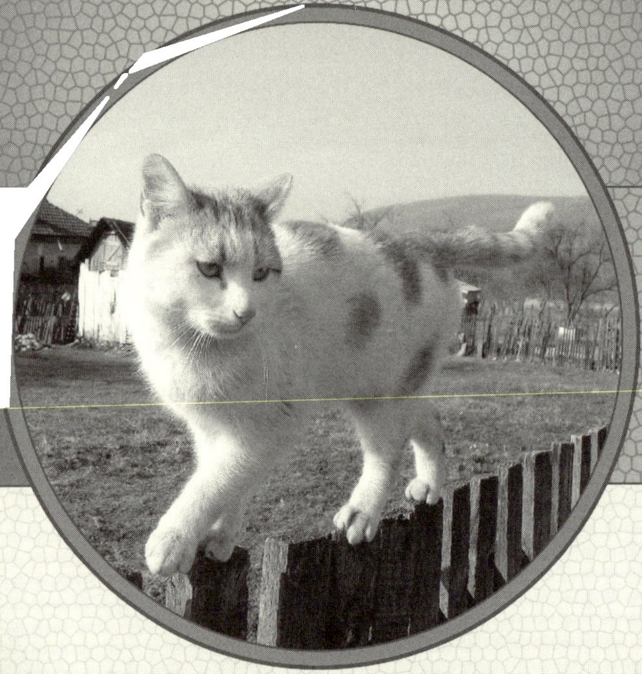

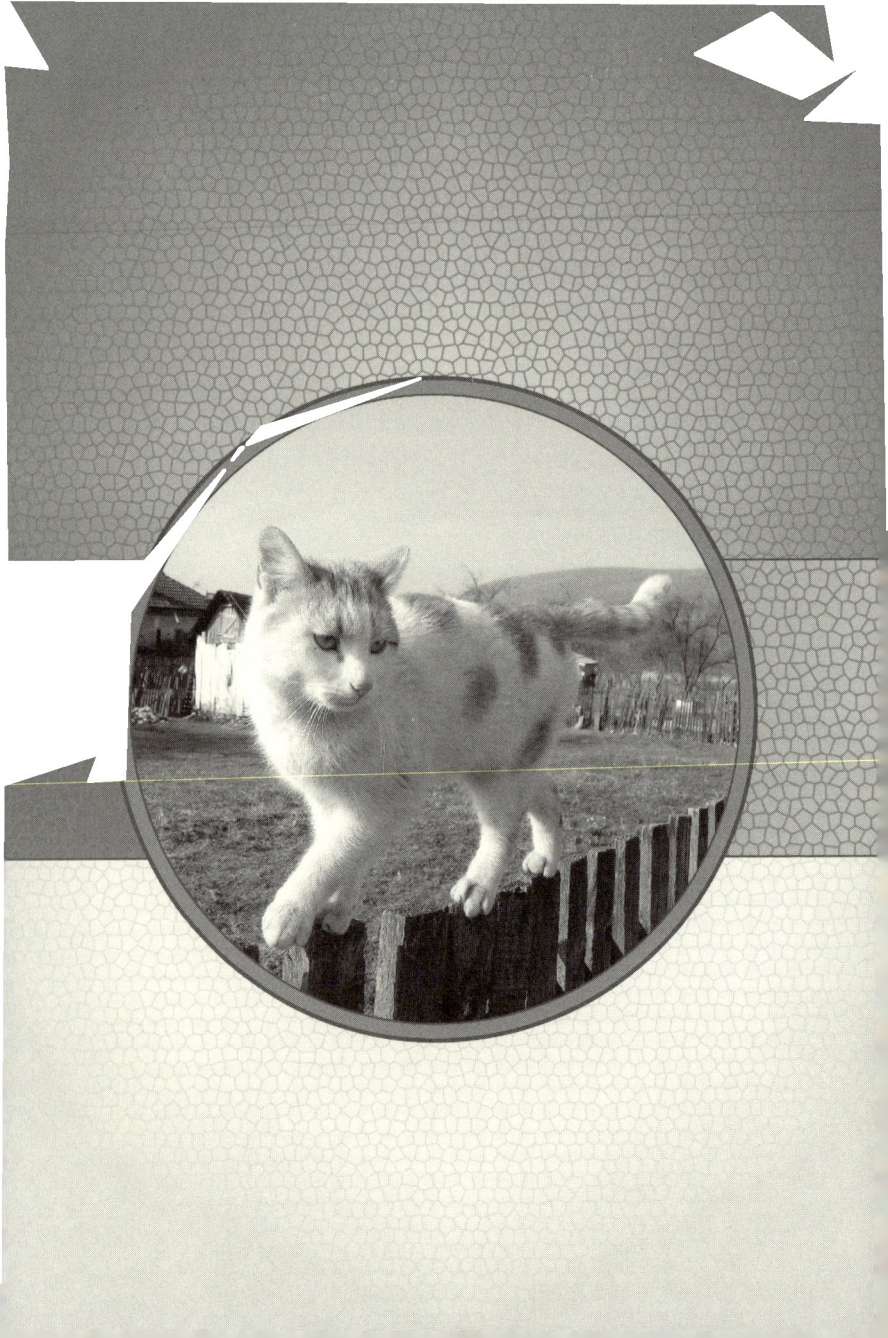

AFTERWORD

*"Other people may be there to help us, teach us,
guide us along our path, but the lesson
to be learned is always ours."*
— Unknown

This book is ending, but the journey continues! Thank you for following the path with me to better health for your feline friend. I know the way is often bumpy and uphill, but the end result is well worth the effort. If the information in this book is new to you and seems overwhelming, please be kind to yourself and have patience. Old patterns sometimes take a little effort to change, but it won't be long before preparing your cat's nutritious new meals becomes just another habit. You may have to keep looking at the recipes at first, just as you would with any new dish, but soon you'll be whipping them up without even a glance. It will be just like making an old family favorite.

You'll notice that I included quite a few variations of raw diets, ranging from whole pieces of meat and bone to totally boneless recipes. I did this because I want to make better nutrition available for all cats, which means that it must be as doable as possible for all humans. Everyone isn't comfortable with the same thing. Some people will feel better (as I do) with feeding whole bones to their cats, but that dictum might cause other individuals to totally shy away from even trying a raw-food diet—and that would be a crime against the feline! I want every cat to have the opportunity to live a long, happy life. So if that means offering different forms of a nutritious raw diet that may appeal to as many of their guardians as possible, then I'm happy to do so. All the recipes provide healthy alternatives to processed pet-food products.

If you feel that you must cook your cat's food, please reread Chapter 7. If you still want to cook, do so only lightly and use Recipe #4, adding the Super Supp, bonemeal, and oils just before serving (don't heat them). You'll need to add a digestive-enzyme product because heat will kill the enzymes found in raw food, and you might also consider using a very good quality amino-acid and multivitamin/mineral supplement because the heat will also destroy many of these nutrients. Even though I prefer feeding a raw diet to cats, if you follow these suggestions, your cooked version will still provide a higher-quality meal than can be found in the typical bag or can of processed pet food.

I must admit that even though my heart ached for those who suffered when the latest massive pet-food recall was announced, I breathed a huge sigh of relief that I didn't have to worry about it affecting my cats. And as I finish writing this book, two new recalls have occurred—no, not the same one I mentioned at the beginning of the book—*new ones.* Once again, I'm relieved that it doesn't affect my beloved animal friends. Even so, it motivates me to help others by writing this book.

This Just In . . .

Talk about synchronicity! As I was putting the final touches on the last draft of this book, I was contacted by the marketing firm for the largest pet-food company in the world (the one that probably has the most influence on many veterinarians). They told me that as a "thought leader" in the nutrition field, they were interested in having me attend a closed session to discuss new marketing tactics for their products. They asked for my opinion on several issues that would be addressed at the meeting.

I must tell you that as I considered the barrage of questions, it occurred to me that they all centered on marketing. They weren't focused on improving the *quality* of the product, but rather on how to best entice you to purchase it. Obviously, this company has felt the heat from the latest pet-food recall, and the ever-growing number of us who feed our animals homemade diets has cut into profits. I attempted to point out the absurdity of some of the questions (like whether they should market special gender products) and tried my best to direct them to the real issues they should address, but that wasn't what they wanted to hear. They were trying to find out what new "niches" could be made and what other gimmicks could be employed to sell more products.

I sought to focus on better-quality ingredients, species-appropriate foods, and what informed guardians want today for their furry family members. Sadly, they weren't interested in this information either; they just wanted to know what sort of advertising would work better on animal lovers. So like it or not, I expect that we'll see some inventive new marketing in the coming year—perhaps special pink kibble for girlie cats! It was a very frustrating experience, and I really do hope that I have another chance to help this company take off their

Afterword

blinders and see what's really needed—not better marketing, better food.

The kibble has hit the fan, my friends, and it's time for things to change. Sharing our lives with cats is a privilege with so many rewards. Living with a species different from ourselves connects us to the natural world unlike anything else. It's a gift that shouldn't be taken for granted. Our cats depend on us to return the favor by taking care of their species-specific needs. With great cats comes great responsibility.

> Health and happiness to you and your feline friends.
> — Kymythy R. Schultze, C.N., C.N.C

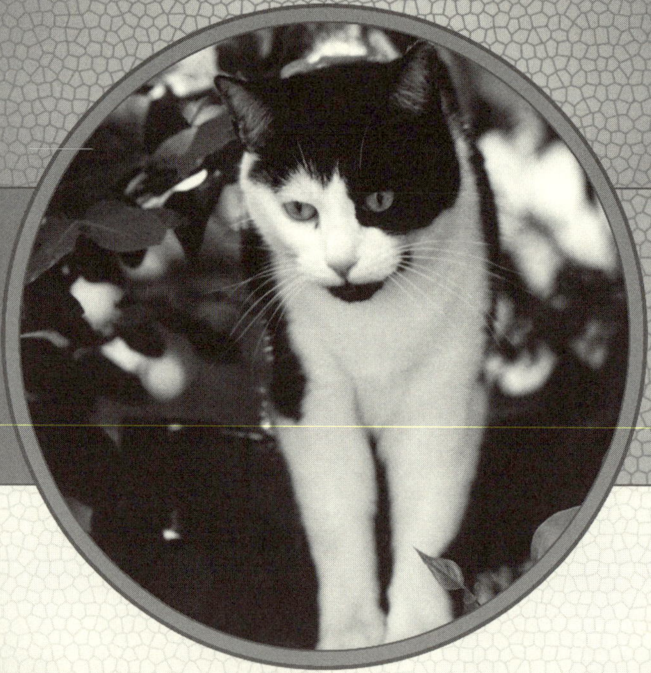

REFERENCES

Animal Protection Institute. "What's Really in Pet Food?" (California: Animal Protection Institute, 1997).

Annual Meeting of the American Association for Cancer Research. *Dangers of Heterocyclicamines* (2000).

Association of American Feed Control Officials Incorporated. *Official Publication* (Atlanta: AAFCO, 2007).

Bauer, J. E. "Fatty Acid Metabolism in Domestic Cats (Felis catus) and Cheetahs (Acinonyx jubatas)" (Proc. Nutr. Soc., 56; 1013-24, 1997).

Belfield, Wendell, D.V.M. "Feline Leukemia: Prevention and Control through Nutritional Immunotherapy" (*Journal of the International Academy of Preventive Medicine,* 40–44, 1983).

Broadhurst, C. Leigh, Ph.D. "The Essential PUFA Guide for Dogs and Cats" (*Nutrition Science News,* Oct. 2001).

Costantini, A., et al. *Diseases caused by Fungi and Their Mycotoxins* (Fungalbionic Series, 1998).

Chong, Daniel H., N.D. "Real or Synthetic: The Truth Behind Whole-Food Supplements" (Mercola, 2005).

Ellis, Chuck, spokesman for the L.A. Sanitation Dept. "L.A. sends 200 tons of euthanized cats and dogs to West Coast rendering every month" (*The New York Times,* Nov. 1997).

Fallon, Sally W., M.A., and Enig, Mary G., Ph.D. "The Ploy of Soy" (California: Price-Pottenger Nutrition Foundation, 1997).

Feingold, B. F. "Hyperkinesis and Learning Disabilities Linked to Artificial Food Flavors and Colors" (*The American Journal of Nursing,* 1975).

"FDA: Pet Food Tainting Might be Intentional" (Associated Press, April 20, 2007).

Greco, Deborah D.V.M. "The 'CatKins' Diet—the Feline Diet: a Historical Look" (AVMA Annual Convention, July 2003).

Hill, A. S.; Werner, J. A.; Rogers, Q. R.; O'Neill, S. L.; and Christopher, M. M. "Lipoic Acid Is 10 Times More Toxic in Cats than Reported in Humans, Dogs or Rats" (*Journal of Animal Physiology and Animal Nutrition,* 88(3–4): 150–56, 2004).

Johnson, Lucy. "Pet Food Cruelty Exposed" (U.K.: *Sunday Express,* Feb. 2004).

References

Logas, D. and Kunkle, G. "Double-blind Study Examining the Effects of Evening Primrose Oil on Feline Dermatitis" (*Veterinary Dermatology,* 4; 181–4, 1993).

Mercola, Joseph, D. O. "Beware—Food is Your Medicine, Not Supplements" (*British Medical Journal,* 328; 211–214, 2004).

Mottram, D. S.; Wedzicha, B. L.; and Dodson, A.T. "Acrylamide is Formed in the Maillard Reaction" (*Nature,* 419/6906; 448–9, 2002).

National Research Council. *Nutrient Requirements of Cats, Revised Edition* (Washington, DC: National Academy Press, 1986).

Ogilvie, G. K. "Nutrition and Cancer: Exciting Advances for 2002" (Proceedings, World Small Animal Veterinary Association, 2002).

Olney, J. W. "Brain Lesions, Obesity, and Other Disturbances in Mice Treated with Monosodium Glutamate" (*Science,* 164:719–721, 1969).

Parker-Pope, Tara. "Why Vets Recommend 'Designer' Chow" (New York: *The Wall Street Journal,* Nov. 1997).

Pet Food Institute *Fact Sheet* (Washington DC: Pet Food Institute, 1994).

Pottenger, Jr., Francis M., M.D. *Pottenger's Cats: A Study in Nutrition* (California: Price-Pottenger Nutrition Foundation, 1983).

Researchers at the Michael Reese Medical Centre. "Nitrates, Nitrites, and Artificial Preservatives to Cancer in Test Subjects" (Victoria, B.C., CNW Group, February 2007).

Robinson, Jo. *Why Grassfed is Best!* (Washington: Vashon Island Press, 2000).

PTCL. "Safety Data for Citric Acid" (Oxford University, 2005)

"Salmonella Declines since HACCP Implementation" *(Journal of the American Veterinary Medical Association,* June 2001).

Scanlan, Richard, Ph.D. "Nitrosamines and Cancer" (The Linus Pauling Institute, 2000).

USDA. "Freezing and Food Safety" (Food Safety and Inspection Service, 2005).

Yu, S., and Gross, K. L. "Moderate Dietary Vitamin C Supplement does not Affect Urinary Oxalate Concentration in Cats" (*Journal of Animal Physiology and Animal Nutrition, vol.* 89; 11–12, 428–429, 2005).

Wayne, Anthony and Newell, Lawrence. "The Hidden Hazards of Microwave Cooking" (**http://www.mercola.com/article/microwave/hazards.htm**, 2003).

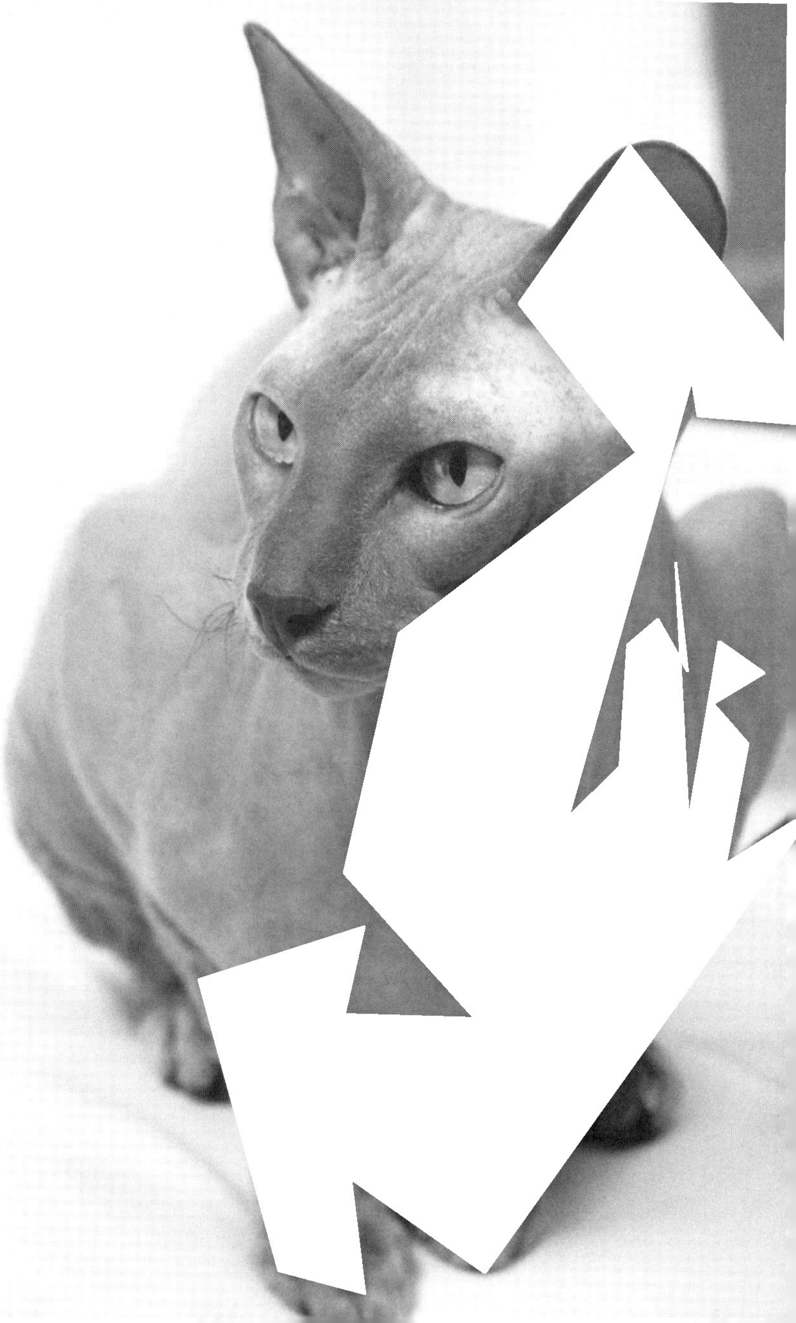

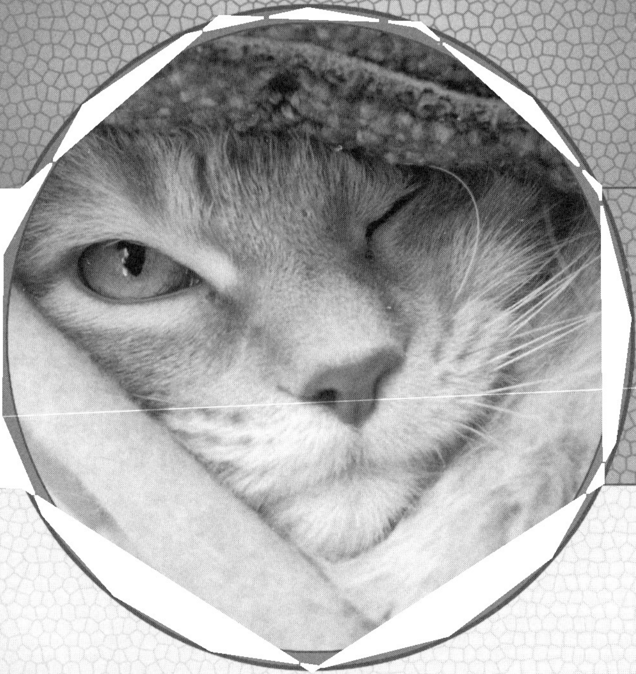

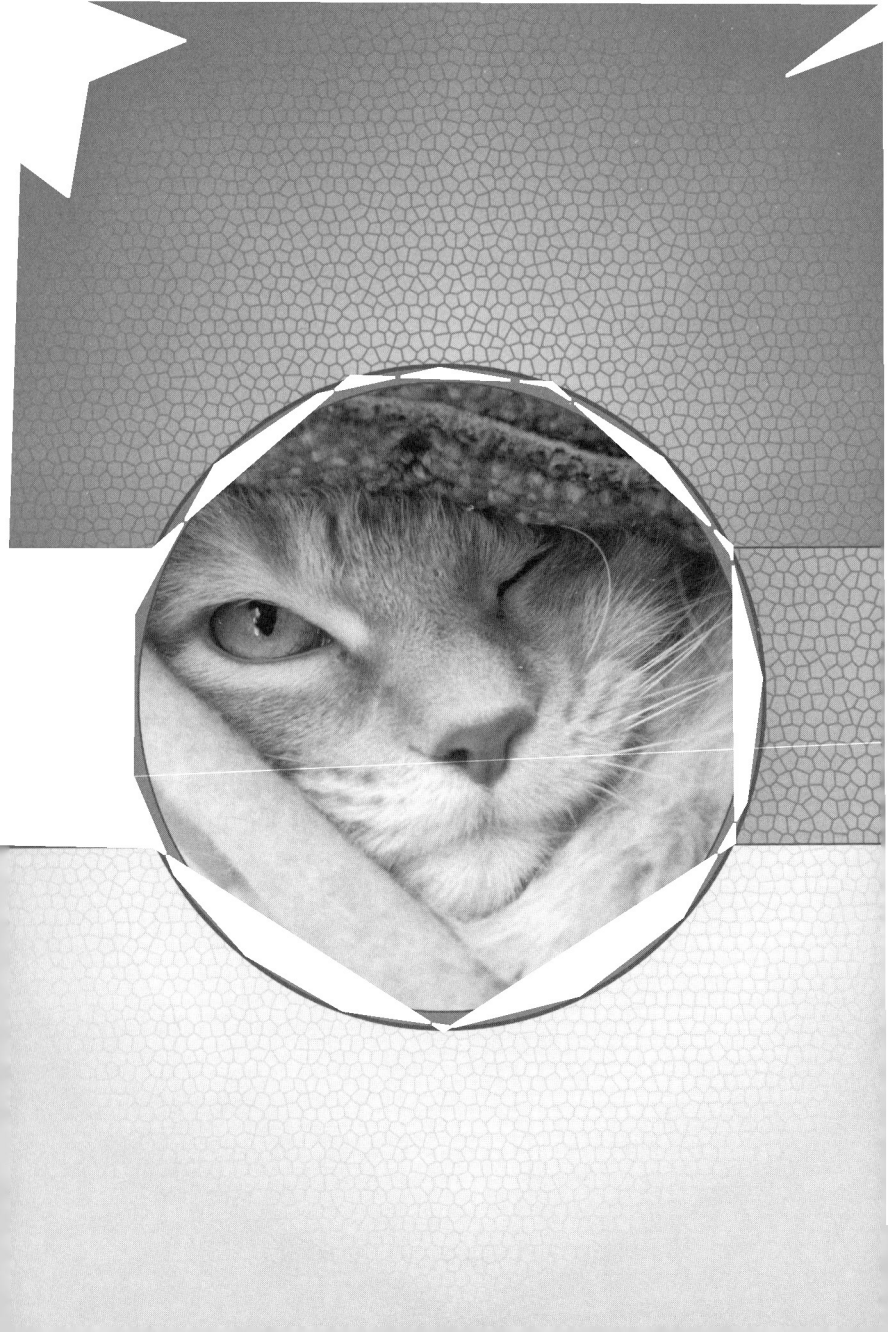

RESOURCES

Here are a few resources that you may find helpful. No endorsements are implied, and I urge you to thoroughly conduct your own research regarding qualifications, compatibility, and quality of health-care providers and products for your cats. Ten years ago, when I wrote my first book on animal nutrition, resources for ingredients, products, and nutritional practitioners were few and far between. Wow, what a difference a decade makes! There are now so many natural health-care and nutrition companies for animals that I can't begin to list them all. In the time it took to write this paragraph, ten more have probably opened for business. Yes, that's how fast the field of natural nutrition and holistic health care for companion animals is growing! For additional resources, check the Internet, your local phone book, human health-food stores, and the ever-growing number of health-food stores specifically for pets.

**The Academy of
Veterinary Homeopathy**
P.O. Box 9280
Wilmington, DE 19809
866-652-1590
theavh.org

AltVetMed:
Complementary
and Alternative
Veterinary Medicine
altvetmed.org

**The American
Academy of Veterinary
Acupuncture**
100 Roscommon Drive,
Suite 320
Middletown, CT 06457
800-632-9911
aava.org

**American Association
of Feline Practitioners**
203 Towne Centre Drive
Hillsborough, NJ
08844-4693
800-874-0498
aafponline.org

**American Holistic
Veterinary Medical
Association**
2218 Old Emmorton Road
Bel Air, MD 21015
410-569-0795
ahvma.org

**American Veterinary
Chiropractic Association**
442154 E 140 Road
Bluejacket, OK 74333
918-784-2231
animalchiropractic.org

**American Veterinary
Naturopathic Association**
P.O. Box 243
Savannah, GA 30275
318-608-4424
avna.us

**Animal Protection
Institute**
P.O. Box 22505
Sacramento, CA 95822
916-447-3085
api4animals.org

**Association of
British Veterinary
Acupuncturists**
abva.co.uk

**Association of Veterinary
Acupuncturists of Canada**
C.P. 73
Beaconsfield

Resources

Québec, Canada H9W 5T6
514-697-0295
avac.ca

Association Scientific Italian Acupuncture Veterinary sans Frontiere
scuoladiagopuntura.it

Australian Veterinary Chiropractic Association
chirovet.com.au

Brazilian Association of Veterinary Acupuncture
komvet.at/ivadkom/
_brazil.htm

British Association of Holistic Nutrition and Medicine
44 (0) 845 465 1056
bahnm.org.uk

British Association of Homeopathic Veterinary Surgeons
Alternative Veterinary Medicine Centre
Chinham House
Stanford in the Vale
Oxfordshire SN7 8NQ
44 (0) 1367 710324
bahvs.com

Chi Institute: Traditional Chinese Veterinary Medicine
9700 West Highway 318
Reddick, FL 32686
800-891-1986
tcvm.com

The Coalition for Natural Health (Animal Dept.)
PMB 100-408
1220 L Street, NW
Washington, DC 20005
800-586-4264
naturalhealth.org

German Veterinary Acupuncture Society
gervas.org

Holistic Animal Therapy Association of Australia
P.O. Box 513
Grafton, NSW 2460
02 66439035
hataa.asn.au

Holistic Health for Animals Association
131 Franklin Plaza #318
Franklin, NC 28734
828-369-8711
holistichealthforanimals
association.com

International Alliance for Animal Therapy and Healing
Route 1 Box 98
Marietta, OK 73448
580-276-9811
iaath.com

International Association of Animal Massage and Bodywork
3347 McGregor Lane
Toledo, OH 43623
800-903-9350
iaamb.org

International Veterinary Acupuncture Society
P.O. Box 271395
Fort Collins, CO 80527-1395
970-266-0666
ivas.org

Netherlands Veterinary Acupuncture Association
snva.nl

New Zealand Holistic Animal Therapists Association
P.O. Box 186
Whangaparaoa
North Auckland
nzhata.org

Price-Pottenger Nutrition Foundation
7890 Broadway
Lemon Grove, CA 91945
800-366-3748
ppnf.org

Veterinary Botanical Medicine Association
1785 Poplar Drive
Kennesaw, GA 30144
vbma.org

Veterinary Institute of Integrative Medicine
P.O. Box 740053
Arvada, CO 80006
303-277-8227
viim.org

The Weston A. Price Foundation
PMB 106-389 4200
Wisconsin Avenue, NW
Washington, DC 20016
202-363-4394
westonaprice.org

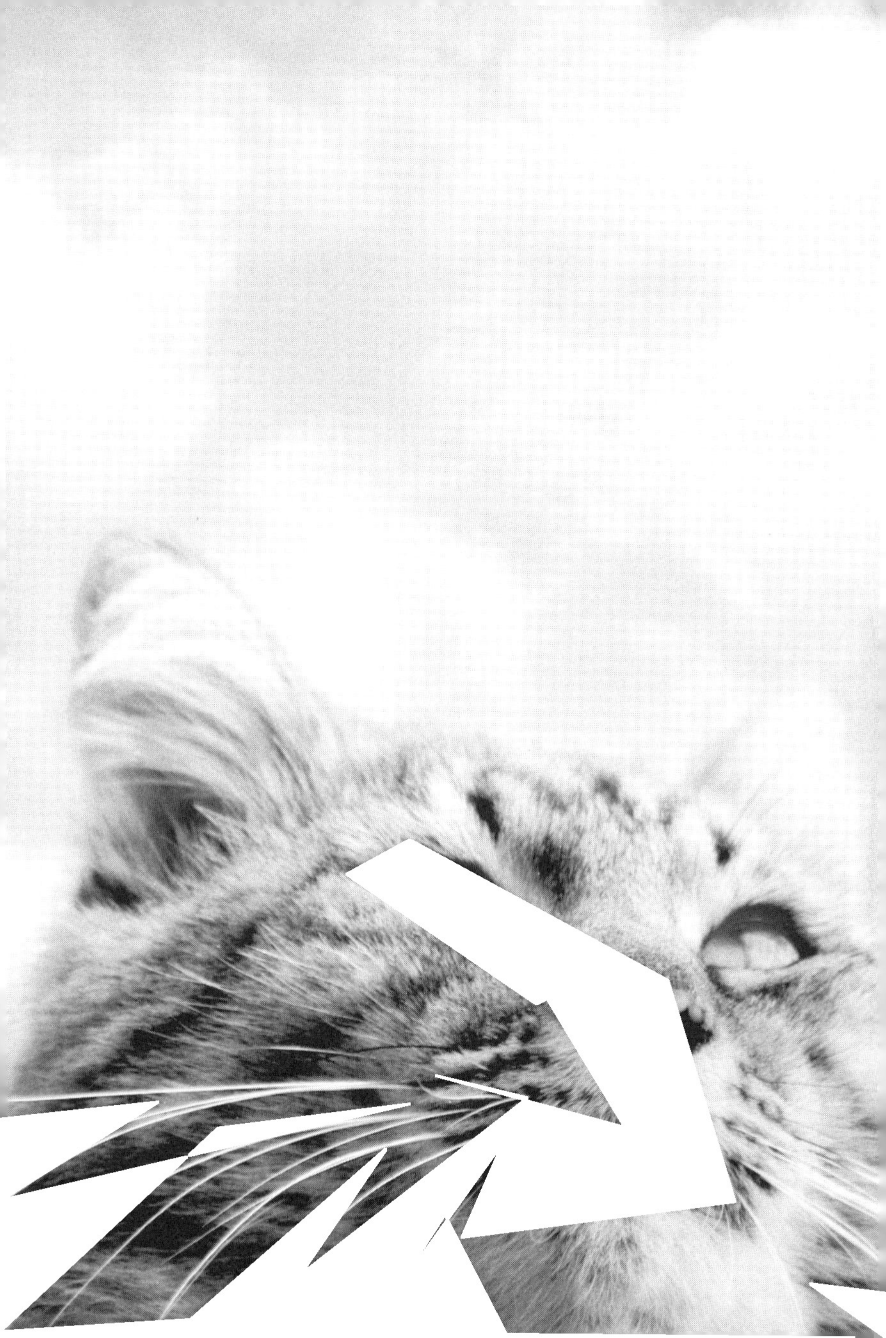

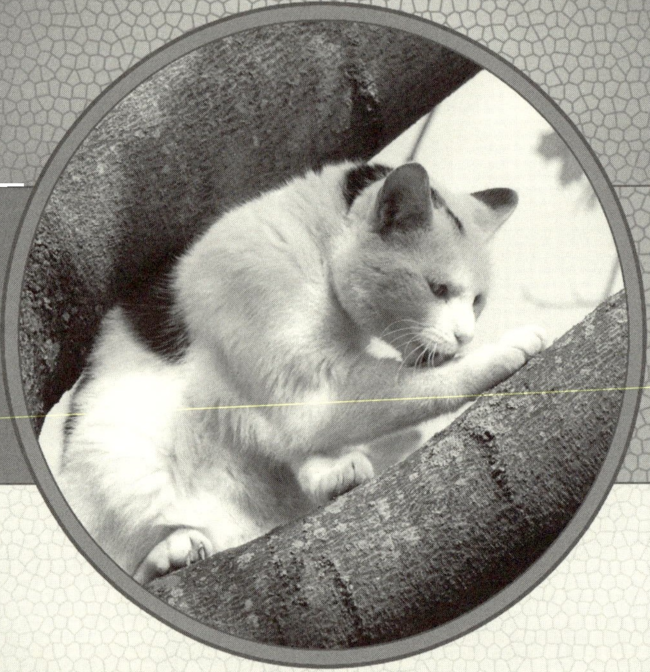

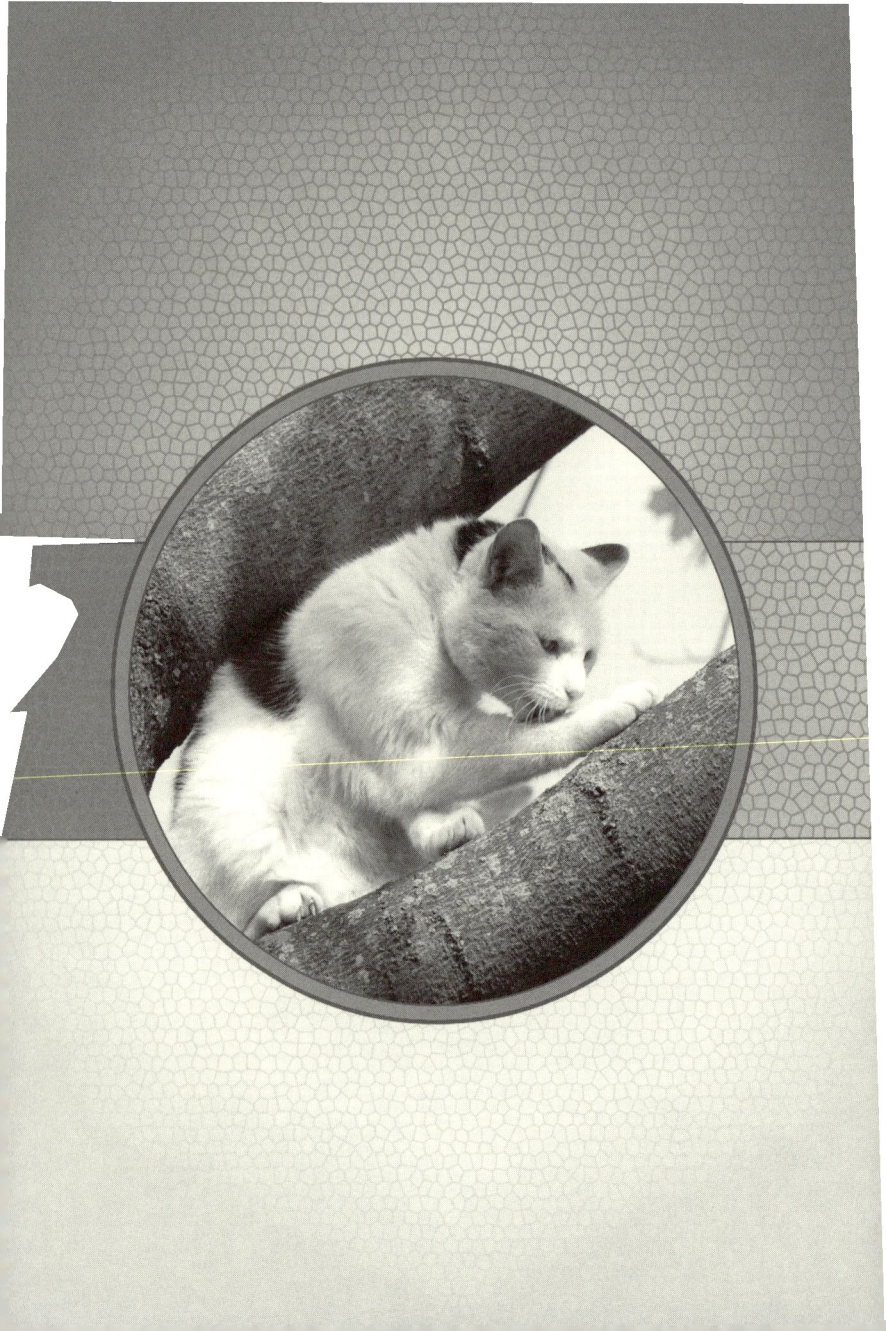

INDEX

4-D animal parts, 41–44, 60

acrylamide, 77
alpha-linolenic acid (ALA), 24–25
alpha lipoic acid (lipoic acid), 143
American Association of Veterinary Laboratory Diagnosticians, 44
Amory, Cleveland, 33
animal fat, 63
Animal Protection Institute, 56
antioxidants, 27
arachidonic acid (AA), 24–25
Aristotle, 161
artificial dyes and flavors, 50
Association of American Feed Control Officials (AAFCO), 34–35
  "complete and balanced" statement, 39–40

Bacon, Francis, xxi
bacteria, raw meat and, 16, 99–103
Bairacli Levy, Juliette de, ix
benzoic acid and related compounds, 51
Berry, Wendell, 49
beta-carotene, 66
BHA and BHT, 51, 63, 65
Blake, Stephen R., Jr., D.V.M., 11
bonemeal, 108, 120
bone(s). *See* raw bone
borage oil, 109, 116, 120, 155
brewer's rice, 62
bribe foods, 130
Burden, Jean, 73

calcium ascorbate, 111, 112, 116, 122, 158
calcium sulfate, 68
cancer
  4-D animal parts and, 42
  acrylamide and, 77
  BHA and BHT and, 51
  heterocyclic amines (HCAs) and, 74
  sodium nitrite and nitrate and, 55–56
  species-appropriate diets and, 5
carbohydrates, 28–29
carnivores, 14–15
casein, 53, 144
C.A.T. diet, 97, 105, 113
  benefits of, 127–28
  caregiver's attitude and, 127
  detox and, 131–32
  feeding, 127
  shopping list for, 116

suggestions for switching to, 129–30
Cauble, Bruce, D.V.M., 13
Centers for Disease Control, 101
chicken, 6, 99, 107, 116, 119, 153–56
   by-product meal, 60–61
   liver flavor, 64
chocolate, 144
chubs, 118
citric acid, 51–52, 63
Clarence and Rosalind (Susan), 7
Cocteau, Jean, 161
"complete and balanced" statement, 39–40
conjugated linoleic acid (CLA), 24–25, 138
corn gluten meal, 63–64
Cornish game hen, 99, 151–53
cornmeal, 61–62

Dahout, Richard, xvii
Dahout, Richard, Dr., xv
dairy, 144
defrosting meals, 130–31
diets for cats, xxii–xxiii, 2
   C.A.T. diet, 97, 113
   cooked meat and, 79–80
   disease and, 136
   ingredient percentages and, 95–97
   pregnancy and lactation and, 136
   processed versus fresh food, 91–97
   seniors and, 137
digestive leukocytosis, 79

disease, 136
dishes, 131
docosahexaenoic acid (DHA), 24–25
domestication, cats and, 16–18
drugs, 53
dulse or kelp powder, 110, 111, 121–22, 158

E. coli, 101
eggs, 151–53, 155–57
eicosapentaenoic acid (EPA), 24–25
Environmental Protection Agency, 77
enzymes, 27–28, 132, 170
   heat and, 77–78
essential fatty acids (EFAs), 24, 109–10
   sources of, 120
essential oils, 145
ethoxyquin, 52–53
evening-primrose oil, 109, 116, 120, 155

fat, 23–25
   feline nutrition and, 24–25
   heat and, 75–76
   saturated versus polyunsaturated, 23
"fat blenders," 45–46
FDA Center for Veterinary Medicine, 52–53
feline digestive systems, 2, 13–16, 78, 99–100
fibrocystic breast disease, xvi
fish-body oil, 109, 116, 151, 153, 155, 157
fish (cod) liver oil, 109

Index

food
   groups, 22–28
   health and, 11–13, 22
   See also diets for cats;
      nutrients
FOS, 102
free-feeding, 126
free radicals, 27

gamma-linoleic acid (GLA),
   24–25, 110
Gandhi, Mahatma, xiii
gelatin, 111, 122
genetic modification, 62, 64
grain(s), ix, 28–29, 145
   cats' nutritional needs
      and, 45, 137–38
   heat and, 76–77
   quality of, 44–45
grapes and raisins, 145
Gray, Charlotte, 125
green tripe, 106

Halley, Emma, Socks, Strider,
   and Jaggers (Fiona), 5–6
Hard Copy, 43
health-food stores, 117, 120,
   121, 139
health problems, 1–2
Heinz bodies, 55
herbs, 146
holism, 161–62
   species-appropriate diets
      and, 162
houseplants, 146

Internet, 112, 117, 120, 121,
   122

Jasper, Matilda, Salte, and
   LeRoy (Erica), 8–9
Johns Hopkins University, 74

kelp and dulse, 110–11
Kliban, B., 85–86
Kouchakoff, Paul, Dr., 78–79

lactobacillus acidophilus,
   102
linoleic acid (LA), 24–25
lipoic acid (alpha lipoic acid),
   143

Maillard, Louis-Camille, 74
malnutrition, 13
McGargle, P. F., Dr., 42
melamine, 44–45
Meridian Valley Laboratory,
   101
microwave ovens, 146–47
minerals, 25, 36
   heat and, 76
   pet-food products and,
      66–68
Molly Mayonnaise (Joyce),
   6–7
MSG (monosodium
   glutamate), 52, 53–54, 64
muscle meat, 98–99
   sources of, 117–18

National Cancer Institute, 74
National Research Council
   (NRC), 75
   Nutrient Requirements of
      Cats, 35–36, 45
   product guidelines and,
      34–39

Subcommittee on Cat Nutrition, 28, 34–39
Natural Nutrition No-Cook Book, The (Schultze), 139
nonfood requirements, 30–31, 139–40
   exercise and sunshine, 162–63
   household chemicals and, 163
   litter box and, 163–64
   vaccines and, 163
Norwegian Veterinary Journal, 112
Nutrient Requirements of Cats (NRC), 35–36, 45
nutrients
   heat and, 97
   synergy and, 21–22, 29–30
   See also diets for cats; food

obesity, cooked food and, 78
onions and garlic, 147
organ meat, 105–6, 151–57
   sources of, 118

pathological leukocytosis, 79
Pecan, El, xviii–xix
pentobarbital, 43
pet-food companies, 5–6
   marketing and, 85–86, 135–36, 171–73
   quality and, 172
   veterinarians and, 83–88
Pet Food Institute, 42
pet-food products, 91–95, 166–67
   "complete and balanced" statement, 39–40
   contents, xiv, 41–46
   dry cat food, 145
   guidelines, 34–39
   shelf-life and, 46–47
   testing, 37–39
   toxins and, xiii–xiv
Pitcairn, Richard, Dr., ix
potassium chloride, 66–68
Pottenger, Francis, Dr., 79–80
pregnancy and lactation, 136
Prevention, 41
Price-Pottenger Nutrition Foundation, 147
probiotics, 102–3, 132
propyl gallate and propylene glycol, 55, 63
protein
   amino acids and, 23, 75
   animal versus vegetable sources of, 23
   heat and, 74–75

Queen Elizabeth Hospital, 74

raw bone, 106–8
   versus bonemeal, 108
   nutrients in, 107
   sources of, 119–20
raw-food studies, 78–81
raw meat
   bacteria and, 16, 99–103
   cultural preferences and, 103
   forms of, 104–5
   preparation of, 104
raw salmon, 99, 147
recalls, pet-food, xiii–xiv, xix, 64, 166, 171

Index

Recipe #1 (Cornish game hen), 151–53
Recipe #2 (ground chicken or boneless parts), 153–55
Recipe #3 (bone-in whole meat), 155–56
Recipe #4 (ground meat), 156–57, 170
Recipe, Super Supp, 158
Resnick, Faith, 59
roadkill, 43

salmonella, 102
salmon, raw, 99, 147
salt, 68
Schweitzer, Albert, 143
seniors, 137–38
Smith, Gary, 83
sodium nitrite and nitrate, 55–56
soy, 147–48
species-appropriate diets
   benefits of, 2–3, 127–28
   cats' anatomy and, 13–16
   health issues and, 1–2
   holism and, 162
   transitioning to, 8
   See also C.A.T. diet
stools, 132
sugar, 148
sunflower seeds, 111
   sources of, 121
Super Supp, 110–12, 116, 151–53, 155, 157
   recipe, 158
supplements, 108–12
   essential fatty acids (EFAs), 109–10
   Super Supp, 110–12

taurine, 22, 65, 105, 107, 166
treats, 138–40
turkey, 98–99, 104, 117
   chubs, 118
Twain, Mark, 1

University of Colorado Health Sciences Center, 102
urinary tract ailments, 2, 5, 7

Valley Proteins, 43
veterinarians
   choosing, 165, 167
   holism and, 164–65
   pet-food companies and, 83–88
   raw-food diets and, 165–66
Vinci, Leonardo da, 135
vitamin-C, buffered powder and, 111–12
vitamins, 25, 36
   beta-carotene and, 66
   heat and, 76
   pet-food products and, 69
Vito and Julius (Sarah), 4

water, 26–27
   heat and, 77
wheatgrass, 139, 146
Wigmore, Ann, 139

yeast, 69, 148

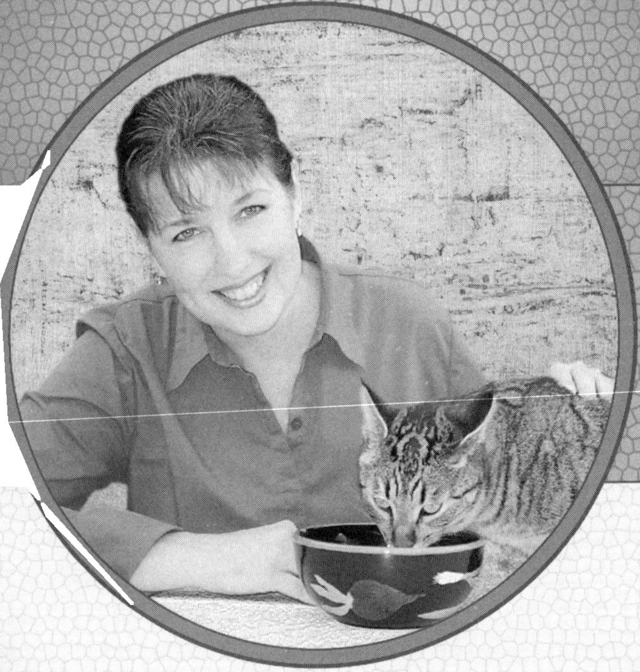

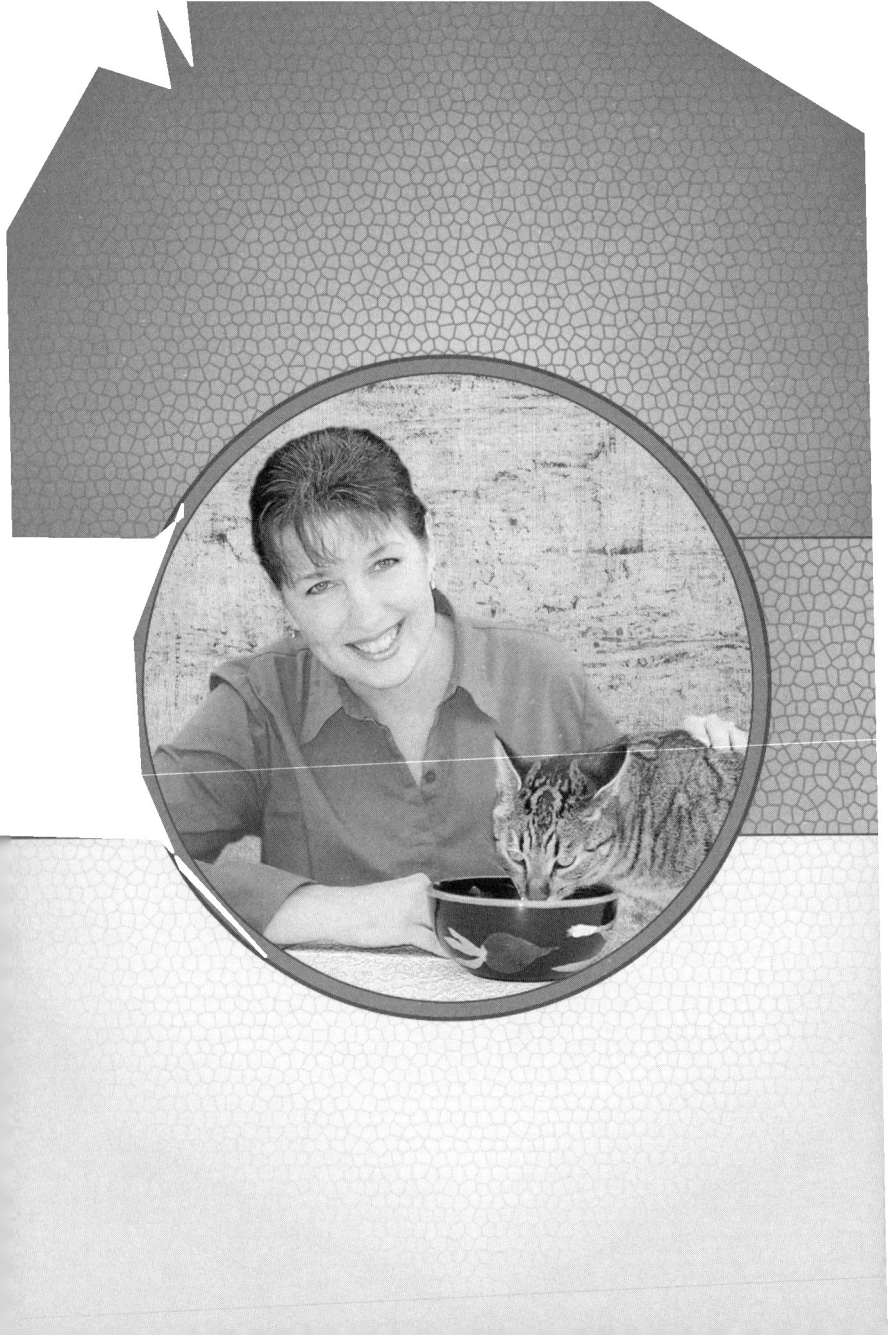

ABOUT THE AUTHOR

Kymythy R. Schultze has been a trailblazer in the field of animal nutrition for more than two decades. She's a Clinical Nutritionist (C.N.) and Certified Nutritional Consultant (C.N.C.). She has been certified as an Animal Health Instructor by the state of California, licensed by the federal government as a Wildlife Rehabilitator, and is a certified Veterinary Orthopedic Manipulation Practitioner (V.O.M.). Kymythy has completed a wide variety of health and nutrition course work, including small-animal nutrition at Cornell University.

In addition to *Natural Nutrition for Cats: The Path to Purr-fect Health,* she's the author of other best-selling books on human and animal nutrition. Her extensive background of formal education and personal experience gave her the insight to be the first to recommend a grainless, species-appropriate diet for cats. Her dietary recommendations are endorsed by veterinarians worldwide and have successfully improved the health and vitality of thousands of cats.

Kymythy lives on a small farm in the Pacific Northwest, and when she isn't lecturing, writing, researching, or consulting, she enjoys preparing healthy and delicious meals for good friends, furry and nonfurry. She's also an enologist (an expert in the science of wine) and winemaker for Gracie Vineyard.

Please visit Kymythy's Website at:
www.kymythy.com.

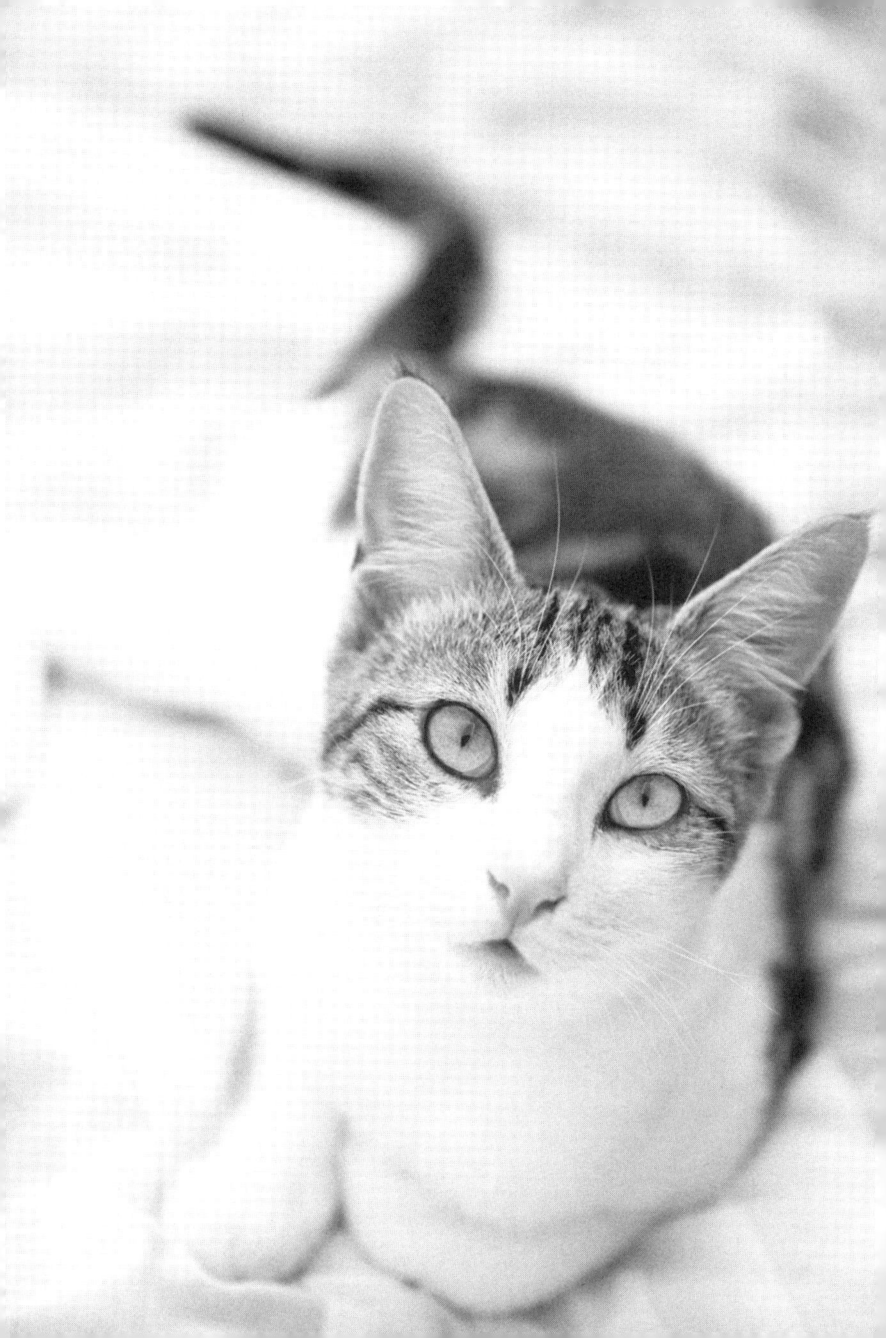

We hope you enjoyed this Hay House book.
If you'd like to receive a free catalog featuring additional
Hay House books and products, or if you'd like
information about the Hay Foundation, please contact:

Hay House, Inc.
P.O. Box 5100
Carlsbad, CA 92018-5100

(760) 431-7695 or **(800) 654-5126**
(760) 431-6948 (fax) or **(800) 650-5115 (fax)**
www.hayhouse.com® • **www.hayfoundation.org**

Published and distributed in Australia by:
Hay House Australia Pty. Ltd., 18/36 Ralph St., Alexandria
NSW 2015 • *Phone:* 612-9669-4299 • *Fax:* 612-9669-4144
www.hayhouse.com.au

Published and distributed in the United Kingdom by:
Hay House UK, Ltd., 292B Kensal Rd., London W10 5BE
Phone: 44-20-8962-1230 • *Fax:* 44-20-8962-1239
www.hayhouse.co.uk

*Published and distributed in the
Republic of South Africa by:*
Hay House SA (Pty), Ltd., P.O. Box 990, Witkoppen 2068
Phone/Fax: 27-11-467-8904 • orders@psdprom.co.za
www.hayhouse.co.za

Published in India by:
Hay House Publishers India, Muskaan Complex,
Plot No. 3, B-2, Vasant Kunj, New Delhi 110 070
Phone: 91-11-4176-1620 • *Fax:* 91-11-4176-1630
www.hayhouse.co.in

Distributed in Canada by:
Raincoast, 9050 Shaughnessy St., Vancouver, B.C. V6P 6E5
Phone: (604) 323-7100 • *Fax:* (604) 323-2600
www.raincoast.com

Tune in to **HayHouseRadio.com**® for the best in
inspirational talk radio featuring top Hay House authors!
And, sign up via the Hay House USA Website to receive
the Hay House online newsletter and stay informed about
what's going on with your favorite authors. You'll receive
bimonthly announcements about Discounts and Offers,
Special Events, Product Highlights, Free Excerpts,
Giveaways, and more!
www.hayhouse.com®

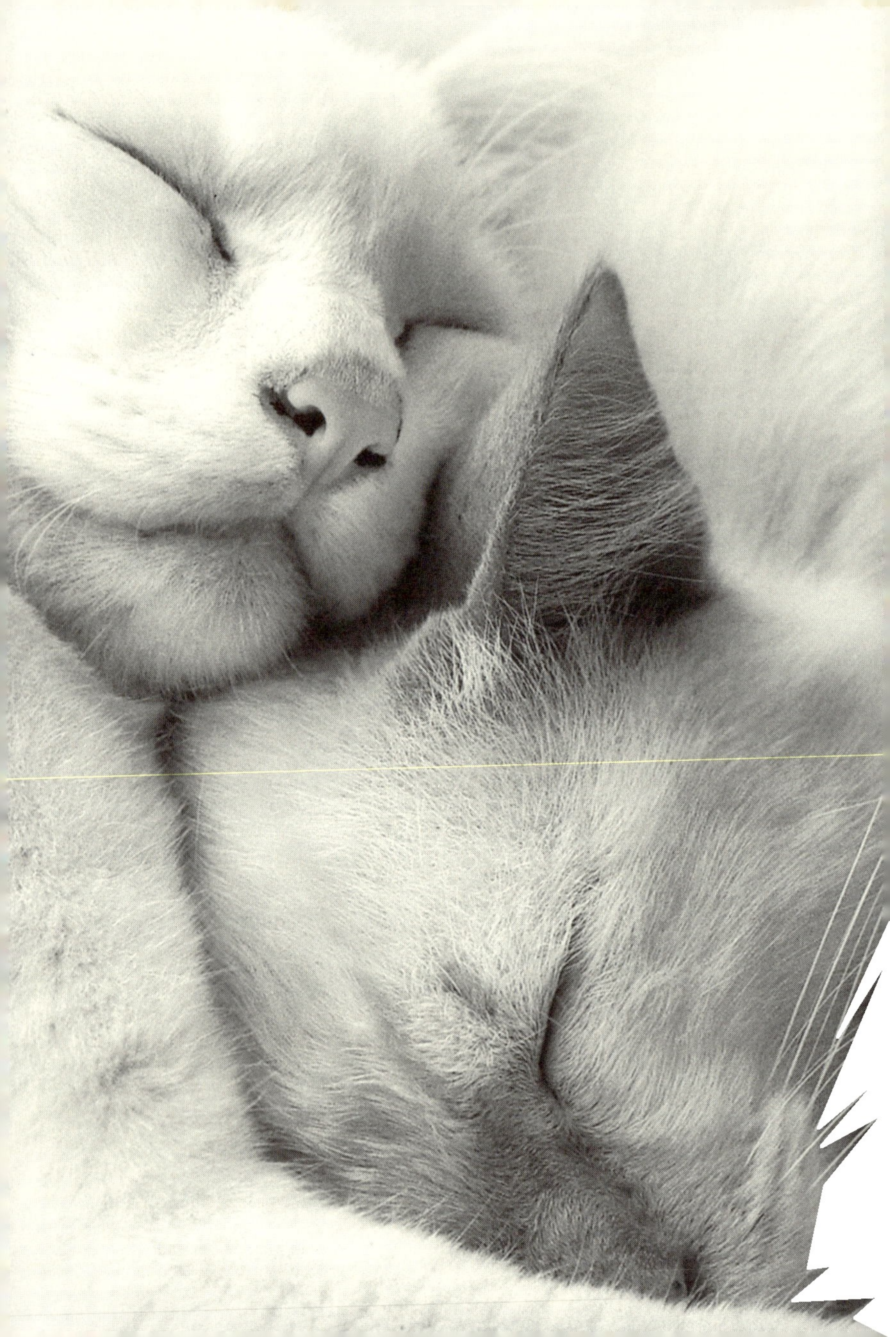